"TO THE GLORY OF GOD, THROUGH
THE LIVES OF
SAINT MARDARIJE
OF LIBERTYVILLE AND CHICAGO
AND **SAINT SEBASTIAN**
OF SAN FRANCISCO AND JACKSON

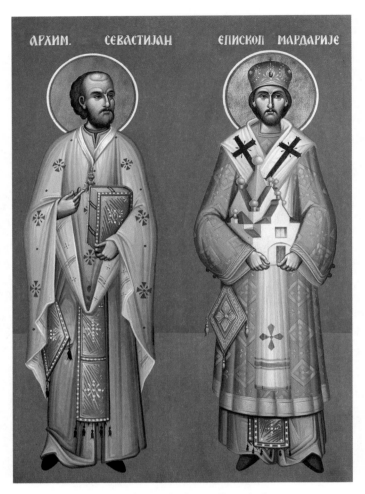

*Saints Mardarije of Libertyville and Chicago
and Sebastian of San Francisco and Jackson.*
Fresco by Leonidas Diamantopoulos at the Holy Resurrection Cathedral in Chicago.

We glorify Thee, O Christ, the King of all, Who by Thine Incarnation didst explain the meaning of all puzzles and images of the Holy Scripture; having come to know the Mystery of Thy Cross and Burial, Thy two new saints, Mardarije of Libertyville and Sebastian of Jackson, explained to Thy people the Mystery of Thine economy; leading the reasonable flock of the Orthodox in America into Thy pasture, enriched by the American Enlighteners; thus initiated into the unspeakable mystery of the Resurrection, they brought us to the knowledge of the purpose for which Thou, O Creator, didst initially bring all into being, glory to Thee!

Sticheron at Lity, Tone 8

"TO THE GLORY OF GOD THE FATHER"

THE LIVES OF
❖ SAINT MARDARIJE ❖
OF LIBERTYVILLE AND CHICAGO
AND ❖ SAINT SEBASTIAN ❖
OF SAN FRANCISCO AND JACKSON

And their selected writings

Sebastian Press
2015

"TO THE GLORY OF GOD THE FATHER"
THE LIVES OF SAINT MARDARIJE
OF LIBERTYVILLE AND CHICAGO AND
SAINT SEBASTIAN OF SAN FRANCISCO AND JACKSON

With the blessing of the Episcopal Council of the Serbian Orthodox
Church in North and South America

Editor-in-Chief:
Bishop Maxim (Vasiljević)

Editors:
Bishop Maxim (Vasiljević),
Hieromonk Damascene (Christensen), Presbytera Ružica Marić

Translators:
Hieromonk Serafim (Baltić), Deacon Marko Bojović

Publishers:
Episcopal Council of the Serbian Orthodox Church
in North and South America, *Sebastian Press*, Western American Diocese,
Interklima-grafika, Vrnjci, Serbia, *Clergy Brotherhood* of the Serbian
Orthodox Church in North and South America

Contemporary Christian Thought series, № 32

Address all correspondence to:
Sebastian Press, 1621 West Garvey Avenue, Alhambra, California 91803

Printed by Interklima-grafika, Vrnjci, Serbia

"To the glory of God the Father" : the lives of Saint Mardarije of Libertyville and
Chicago and Saint Sebastian of San Francisco and Jackson and their selected writings /
editor-in-chief: Bishop Maxim (Vasiljević) ; editors: Bishop Maxim (Vasiljević), Hieromonk Damascene (Christensen), Presbytera Ružica Marić ; translators: Hieromonk
Serafim (Baltić), Deacon Marko Bojović. — Alhambra, California : Episcopal Council of
the Serbian Orthodox Church in North and South America ; Sebastian Press ; Clergy
Brotherhood of the Serbian Orthodox Church ; Interklima-grafika, 2015.

pages ; cm.

(Contemporary Christian thought series ; no. 31)

ISBN: 978-1-936773-23-7

1. Mardarije, Bishop, 1889–1935. 2. Dabovich, Sebastian. 3. Christian saints—Orthodox Eastern Church—Biography. 4. Orthodox Eastern Church—Clergy—Biography.
5. Orthodox Eastern Church—Doctrines. I. Vasiljević, Maksim, 1968– II. Damascene,
Hieromonk, 1961– III. Marić, Ružica. IV. Serafim, Hieromonk. V. Bojović, Marko.
VI. Series.

BX393 .T6 2015   2015945625
281.9/0922—dc23   1508

CONTENTS

Concerning Orthography

Note on the spelling and pronunciation
of Serbian words and names

Ć ć—not to be found precisely in English: a sound between
the English *t* in tune, and *ch* in chalk

C c—as English *ts* in lots

Č č—as English *ch* in church

Đ đ—as English *j* in jack

Dž dž—as English *j* in George

J j—as English *y* in yell

Lj lj—as English *li* in million

Nj nj—as English *n* in new

Š š—as English *s* in ship

Ž ž—as English *s* in pleasure, or French *j* in jour

FOREWORD

by Patriarch Irinej of the Serbian Orthodox Church

THIS BOOK contains hagiographies of the two newly canonized Saints of the Church on the North American continent, who as the offspring of the Serbian nation have brought to the feast of the entire Orthodox Church their most beautiful personal gifts and the gifts of their people (cf. Rev. 11:10).

The main impetus for the publishing of this hagiographic work came from the desire to rekindle the memory of the God-pleasing personalities of Mardarije of Libertyville and Sebastian of Jackson, exactly now at the time of many jubilees tied to them. Inspired with the decision and support of the Episcopal Council of the Serbian Orthodox Church in North and South America, the writers of these two hagiographies have put together these two short works.

Sanctity in the Church has never been reduced to a conceptual dimension, but it has always striven toward the experience and the vision of God in Trinity. The mystery of the Church is for the saints a living reality of the presence of the incarnate and resurrected God-man Christ—through experience—in church services, revelation, relics, holy icons, and words inspired by the Holy Spirit in the Holy Scripture and in the great teachers of the Church, and in the transformational mutual relationship between asceticism and prayer.

In this decade we commemorate several important dates here on the North American continent; and before any others, the 95th anniversary of the founding of the first Serbian Diocese of America and Canada for the "new" continent is commemorated. This founding of our diocese has elevated the life of our compatriots and our Church to a traditional episcopal and diocesan level. It is in the image of Bishop Mardarije Uskoković, the first Serbian bishop on this continent, that the deep common longing of our ancestors who immigrated to the New World was crowned in a most beautiful way. They courageously decided to set out for a foreign land, not hesitating because of the inevitable difficulties that would come, but going forward inspired by their deep faith, their Orthodox Church identity, and their honorable ancestral heritage. They felt and knew that loyalty to the Church and the unwavering fight for the building of the community and for the integration of oneself into the organism of the community are far more important than personal interests and ambitions.

With care for the awareness of the importance of unity, which they inherited from their old country, our ancestors assembled here, in the beginning oftentimes forming parishes together with our Russian and Greek Orthodox brothers, always remaining open and ready to witness evangelical love for their new non-Orthodox neighbors. Difficult circumstances in the Church life in America prompted our ecclesiastical pioneers to unite and strengthen our Church communities by electing a first bishop for Canada and America. This first stage of the thorny path toward ecclesiastical unity, in which Saints Nikolai Velimirović, Mardarije Uskoković, and Sebastian Dabović were greatly involved, has produced its fruit precisely in recent times, as it allowed for a complete overcoming of the administrative disagreements of our dioceses. Among many other laborers in this field, all of whom are known to God, we should point out the merits of Saint Varnava (Nastić) of Hvostno. For the sake of further strengthening and establishing our Church life and witness in America, it is necessary to declare the unity of all Orthodox people through keeping communion with each other; and for this purpose the bishops of all Orthodox peoples in America have been working together in a common episcopal assembly for North America.

A unique characteristic of the celebrating of the men and women pleasing to God is a specific spiritual-charismatic component which the Liturgical assembly assumes, thanks to the grace-giving iconic presence of the saints, and oftentimes due to the actual presence of their venerable and holy relics. The gathered people hear the festive service, the hymns that were composed and set to music by sacred hymnographers. New icons are written and displayed for veneration, and vigils and services are served. In this way all the members of the Church can show their respect and veneration for the saints: through prayer and Liturgy, through praising them in new hymns, by contemplating their images in the new icons, by venerating the relics of their incorrupt bodies, and by participating in all-night vigils and consecrations of local churches dedicated to their names and images.

May the memory of the two Saints and the jubilees that we celebrate in America remind all of us of the diligence of our ancestors and direct all of us toward the sacred goal of unity in Christ in His Orthodox Church.

We are thankful for the help of Sebastian Press, the publishing house of the Diocese of Western America.

I
Saint Mardarije
of Libertyville and Chicago

St. Sava Serbian Orthodox Monastery   Libertyville, Illinois

The Life of Bishop Mardarije
of Libertyville and Chicago

*A New Equal-to-the-Apostles Father
of the Orthodox Church in America and Canada*

✠

*Therefore I endure all things for the sake of the elect,
that they also may obtain the salvation
which is in Christ Jesus with eternal glory.*
(2 Tim. 2:10)

T HE LIVES of the saints of Christ are woven into the *church of the first-born who are registered in heaven* (Heb. 12:23). The example of their lives, characterized by crucifixion and resurrection and all of their deeds, sufferings and testimonies, even though *hidden with Christ in God* (Col. 3:3), are revealed like a meteor in the sky of the Church, when *the fullness of the time* (Gal. 4:4) comes, in order to illumine the entire sacred history of salvation in those lands to which God the Lord Himself personally led them. The sound of their message of crucifixion and resurrection, and the sound of their testimonies, has been heard throughout the whole world and has leavened all of the dough of history, attracting people to the Church of Christ from the East to the West and from the North to the South.

The Serbian Orthodox Church was faced with many trials in the 20th century, which are hard to enumerate. One of the greater such trials was both the voluntary and involuntary emigration of the

Serbian people from their native lands, all the way from the East to the West. And still this in itself contained a great blessing, personified in many known and unknown Christians who have become Christ-like. Aside from the two great bishops, Saint Nikolai of Žiča (+1956) and Saint Varnava of Hvostno (+1964), and also aside from the holy hieromonk Sebastian of Jackson (+1940), another person given to us by God to keep, to maintain, and to deepen the authentic life in Christ—yet in the Serbian style and experience, a person who lived the covenant of Saint Sava and the covenant of Kosovo, the same covenant that Serbs who were coming carried with them— is the person of the first Serbian bishop in America and Canada, Mardarije Uskoković (+1935).

All the four above-mentioned saints who lived in the diaspora *entered by the narrow gate* and went in by *the difficult way, which leads to life* (Mat. 7:13-14), with faith but also with great struggle, sowing the seed of the Gospel—the word of the Living God. And they did this in the diaspora, where man, from the earliest known times, had always eaten his bread *in the sweat of his face* (Gen. 3:19) more than in the homeland. The diaspora unceasingly "reminds us that the Church in this world and this age has the status of a pilgrim and the status of one who has to be crucified: 'we are in the world, but we are not of the world'....... The Kingdom of God is already present, but we are still on the path to that Kingdom, to our Heavenly Fatherland."[1]

The Providence of God has given to the Serbian Orthodox people in the diaspora

> to recognize, for the time being, the four great strands of prayer, which have led them during the 20th century as authentic visionaries and as true prophets and illumined the path of all those laborers who came from the motherland, which is to say, at the time, from all the parts of Yugoslavia. The fourth strand, or to be more correct, the first one chronologically, Bishop Mardarije (Uskoković), during his life in the Holy Spirit, was not only a true pillar for the Orthodox Serbs in America and Canada, but he is and will be—much more in the time which is ahead of us,

---

[1] Bishop Atanasije (Jevtić), *Contemporary Ecclesiological Reminder on the Diaspora* (Los Angeles-Vrnjci, 2013), p. 9.

as is always the case with all the saints of the Church of God, through His Providence.[2]

It is not easy to approach writing about the earthly life of a *"Christ-like, truth-loving and divinely righteous"* character (according to the words of his contemporary Božidar Purić, Consul General) as was hieromonk and later Bishop Mardarije Uskoković (1889-1935).[3] "If he wanted to become a monk at the age of eleven, then this story is not an accidental one."[4] And there are many other moments from his life, which were not the fruit of chance. This description of his life records some of them.

※

Mardarije was born as Ivan P. Uskoković, on November 2, 1889, in the hilly and stony village of Kornet, in the *nahija* [an administrative unit—trans.] of Lješani, in Montenegro. He was baptized in the village church dedicated to Saint George and his baptismal name was Ivan. Near that church, in the very village of Kornet, there used to be a monastery from the time of the Nemanjić Dynasty, according to tradition. The ruins and a part of the walls, the fortification of the monastery, exist to this day. As the most notable family in the *nahija* of Lješani, characterized by its bravery and nobility, Ivan's ancestors, the Uskokovići, had lived for centuries within the grounds of this expansive and fortified monastery.

Mardarije's father was called Petar (nickname: Pero), and his mother Jela was from the well-known house of Božovići. In Montenegro, Petar was a respected governor of the *nahija* of Lješani and a tribal captain. His great-grandfather, the councilor of the People's Assembly (senator), Duke Stanko (nickname: Stano) Uskoković,

---

[2] Ružica Marić, *Holy Bishop Mardarije Uskoković: The First String of the Covenant of Saint Sava and Kosovo in America and Canada* (book in manuscript) (Libertyville, Ill., 2015), p. 29.

[3] Major information on his life and episcopal work is found in the Archive of the Serbian Orthodox Church in North and South America, which is kept in Saint Sava Monastery in Libertyville, Illinois, and at the see of the Bishop of New Gračanica and Midwestern America, as well as in the book of Dragutin Dragutinović, *The Life of Bishop Mardarije* (New Gračanica, 1992). The subjects in the Archive do not yet have catalogue numbers.

[4] Metropolitan Amfilohije (Radović), *Sermon at the Annual Memorial Service for Bishop Mardarije (Uskoković)*.

Saint George Church, where Ivan Uskoković was baptized and chrismated.

Within the walls of this monastery, the Uskoković family
lived in a house for centuries.

St. Sava Monastery in Libertyville, Illinois.

Hieromonk Mardarije (1920s).

was a well-known hero during the reign of Saint Petar of Cetinje—
Petar I Petrović Njegoš—and the commanding officer of the army
of Montenegro against the French conquerors, who led by Napo-
leon set off on expedition to defeat the small Montenegro, the faithful ally of Russia. Duke Stanko died in the battle at Dubrovnik in
1813. His story was sung by the bishop and ruler of Montenegro,
Petar II Petrović Njegoš, in his well-known "*Slobodijada*" ("*The Tale
of Freedom*").

Since he was from a well-known family, Ivan P. Uskoković, un-
like many of his peers, was sent to become educated. First, he attended elementary school in Rijeka Crnojevića, and then the school
in Cetinje, the capital of Montenegro. "As an eleven-year-old boy,
he asked the Metropolitan of Montenegro Mitrofan to tonsure him
as a monk. When they refused him and did not understand him, he
took off with his brother Ilija and went to Belgrade to get more
education."[5]

His education continued at the high school in Belgrade [the
high school then would be equivalent to the middle school and high
school as we know them today in America—trans.]. Already in the
5th grade of the school that he was in, by his sincere desire to follow
Christ, a desire that he had known from the earliest days of his childhood, Mardarije resembled the youth from the Gospel, who (in the
words of Saint Justin of Ćelije) asked Christ the most radical question: "*How do I gain eternal life?*" At his enthronement as the first
Bishop of America and Canada (April 15, 1926, at the Cathedral in
Belgrade), he reminisced about the days of his youth, when he as a
poor student walked around the Cathedral in Belgrade with the
desire to live his entire life for the Church. On that occasion, he
thanked the gray-haired Patriarch Dimitrije of the Serbian Orthodox Church, from whose hand he received the bishop's staff, for his
goodness exhibited towards this little student from Montenegro.

> The Metropolitan at the time Dimitrije... noticed even then a
> wondrous glow in the eyes of the boy from the mountains of
> Montenegro, and he fulfilled his request. He gave him a letter with

---

[5] D. Dragutinović, *Životopis Vladike Mardarija (The Life of Bishop Mardarije)* (New
Gračanica, 1992), p. 52.

a warm recommendation to Bishop [of Žiča] Sava at Studenica Monastery to receive him; and Vladika Sava did receive him and, after three months of novitiate and three more months of waiting, tonsured him.[6]

After nine years of schooling and without the knowledge of his parents, after a relatively short period of novitiate due to his Christ-like image, he was already tonsured at the Serbian Lavra of Studenica, the endowment of the Nemanjići from the 12th century. "His parents did not know about this and they considered that they had lost their son through misfortune."[7] At his tonsure he received the name Mardarije, with which he continued his life.

Just like Saint Sava in his day, Ivan became a monk against the will of his parents and gave his youth in its entirety to the cross-bearing love of Christ. A folk poet described the beginning of his life on the path of Saint Sava with the following words:

> He dropped the toy from his boyish hand,
> And fled into the night from his father's haven;
> In Studenica he received his black robe,
> And entirely gave himself to prayer.[8]

He heard the voice of God early in his youth, and therefore he heard it deeply in his *heart* (an Old Testament expression, which encompasses the entire man), to which he responded by receiving the monastic order, fully dedicating himself to the service of the God-man Jesus Christ and offering entirely to Christ the most precious thing one can offer—his own life.

※

In 1905 the Holy Synod of the Serbian Orthodox Church decided to send the young Hierodeacon of the Metropolitanate of Montenegro, Mardarije, to be fur-

Hierodeacon Mardarije (Uskoković).

[6] Ibid., p. 52.
[7] Ibid., p. 52.
[8] Ibid., p. 157.

ther educated in Russia. Initially, the Synod "wanted to send him to be educated in Bern, Switzerland, at the Old Catholic University, where several of our bishops had been educated, but at the request of Mardarije himself, he was sent instead to the spiritual academy in Saint Petersburg."[9]

Initially, in September of 1906, he went to Zhitomir spiritual seminary, near Kiev, Ukraine. After two school years, in 1908, he went to Kishinev spiritual seminary in Moldavia. In 1908 he became a hieromonk and in 1912 became a synkellos.[10] He finished the spiritual seminary in Kishinev in 1912, with the best of grades. Immediately afterwards, he enrolled in the spiritual academy in Saint Petersburg, which he finished in 1916, receiving his degree in theology.

Aside from theological studies, Mardarije also studied church law at the law school in Saint Petersburg, which would prove to be especially important and useful in his later work in America and Canada.

Every day of his 12-year stay in Russia (1905–1917), he was imbued with a national, political struggle for the realization of the pan-Slavic idea—the union of all Slavs. Even as a nineteen-year old, in the time of the annexation of Bosnia and Herzegovina, with the voice of an Old Testament prophet of God he started to warn the Russian people of the danger of Germanization. Let us mention two reasons which inspired him to never give up, even after he acquired enemies, some of whom were even in the royal court. First, hieromonk Mardarije continued to build on the foundations of the Slavic, or rather Serbian-Russian, union, which was established in the 12th century by the Russian monks who took the young Rastko, our Saint Sava, and tonsured him in the Russian monastery of Saint Panteleimon on the Holy Mountain. Second, he was continuing the struggle of his ancestors of at least the previous two centuries, who were fighting for the realization of "that fateful and grand idea, Pan-Slavic unity" (Bishop Mardarije, 1916). Like Saint Nikolai of Žiča (at least in one period of his life), he was a pan-Slavist in the greatest sense of the word. "It was on that topic that I wrote my academic

---

[9] Bishop Dionisije, "Short Biography of Bishop Mardarije," in *Spomenica (Memorial Book)*, (Libertyville: Saint Sava Monastery, 1953), p. 59.

[10] In Greek, σύγκελλος, lit. "living in the same cell. " Originally this meant serving as a cell-attendant to a bishop.—Ed.

work for receiving of my degree,"[11] said Bishop Mardarije on one occasion.

His expansive work on the question of the union of all Slavic people (*"to be or not to be"*) was supported by many, but it also led to him gaining a certain number of enemies.... Father Mardarije was under the impression that such an opinion (anti-Slavic) was not just held by Rasputin (who told him on one occasion, "Go to hell you and your Serbs! Let the Germans do with them whatever they want!"), but also in the whole society around him (Rasputin)... whose strings were pulled around the unfortunate Empress Alexandra, who naively, deeply, and sincerely believed that her sick son, the heir to the throne, Alexei, for whose disease there was no cure, could only be saved by the "man of God," Rasputin.[12]

When one of his friends in Russia asked him to explain his plans, filled with immeasurable love and boundless faithfulness to Christ the Savior and His Body—the Church—to his Faith, the original, the ancestral Faith, Hieromonk Mardarije answered simply:

Sowing Christian love,
spreading peace,
quieting passions,
preaching good, and
turning people into brothers.[13]

The humiliated and insulted had a special place in his heart, or rather, the first place. He characterized the gift of mercy as being one of the greatest gifts that he received from God. All of his life was woven with mercy for those who were in need, who were sent to him by God Himself in such great numbers. This is why his daily almsgiving was immeasurable. There is much that will remain for us a secret forever, which only the Most High God will know. From the information about his stay in Russia, we would like to quote, for example, that he used to visit prison camps in Siberia, Turkestan, and Bukhara, where he would encourage and have conversations with prisoners who were Slavs from Austro-Hungary. Regarding that period, the poet writes the following lines about Mardarije:

---

[11] Dragutinović, p. 17.
[12] A newspaper from Saint Petersburg on November 21, 1916, in Dragutinović, p. 20.
[13] Dragutinović, p. 12.

In Russia he saw the simple and the rich,
He saw the paupers' sheds and the palaces of emperors,
But nothing led him astray from the path
On which God and God's work is celebrated.[14]

At the same time, he carried in his soul the burden of the tie to his motherland his whole life. He managed, for example, to collect about three hundred thousand rubles for help for Montenegro.[15] The bountiful deeds of mercy *for the life of the world* of Bishop Mardarije Uskoković we are going to leave for the very end, when his Christ-like image will reveal itself in its fullness among his Serbian people in America and Canada.

The last year of the stay of Synkellos Mardarije in Russia, which was 1917, was marked by his election as a lecturer at the Slavic Gymnasium of Professor Gribovsky in Saint Petersburg, as well as by his participation (as a delegate), also in Saint Petersburg, in the All-Russian Church Assembly, in which Saint Tikhon the Confessor (+1925) was elected to be the patriarch.

During his stay in Russia, Mardarije wrote several books, of which the most important, perhaps, are *The Quiet Corner of Christ*, *Collected Sermons*, and *The Message to the Russian People*.[16] In this last book he called on the Russian people to rise to the defense of Serbs, which would (as in many times in the past) cause protests among the enemies of the pan-Slavic idea, the Russian Germanophiles.

The hard missionary work which Mardarije had started in Russia, he continued in the even more distant America. Namely, led by the Holy Spirit, the Holy Synod of the Russian Orthodox Church decided on July 3, 1917, to send the proven servant of God of the Serbian race, the young synkellos Mardarije Uskoković, to America for the sake of implementing the much-needed organization of the Serbian Church there and for the sake of conducting authentic missionary work among the Serbs in distant North America.[17] The Ho-

---

[14] Ibid., p. 157.

[15] "Hieromonk Mardarije," *The Dawn of Russia*, July 20, 1916, in Dragutinović, p. 12.

[16] The entire income from his book *The Quiet Corner of Christ* he gave to the poor in Russia.

[17] The Russian Ministry of Foreign Affairs (Kerensky's Provisional Government) issued him a passport on July 17, 1917, since he was a Russian citizen, but under the condition that he would immediately leave for America; in Dragutinović, p. 33.

ly Hierarchical Synod sent him to work within the boundaries of the Russian Church Mission and to govern the Serbian mission in America so that he could continue his life in Christ there because "the time was ripe to present to the Serbian people the idea that they should govern their own church life in America..." The chosen one was "a Serb, Father Mardarije Uskoković, who was appointed as the head of the Serbian Mission in America and who received the duty of calling together an ecclesiastical assembly, of the priests and laity, for the sake of the organization of the Serbian Orthodox Church in America."[18] Mardarije arrived in America through Siberia and Vladivostok at the end of 1917, as we shall see, as a "prepared whole-burnt offering" (*The Martyrdom of Polycarp*, 14:1).

Bishop Mardarije spent the most important part of his apostolic, pastoral life and work in North America, where he continued to gather sheaves of spiritual wheat, preparing them for the eucharistic harvest, sacrifice and table within the Serbian Orthodox Church there.

Mardarije as a hierarch.

[18] Dragutinović, p. 33.

The first bishop-administrator of the Serbian Orthodox Church in America and Canada was the Holy Bishop Nikolai of Ohrid and Žiča, who recommended Hieromonk Mardarije Uskoković to be the administrator of the Diocese of America and Canada. How justified this suggestion was will be shown through the suffering, cross-bearing life of Bishop Mardarije. Bishop Mardarije was a God-seeker, a priest, a patriot, an enlightener *in the image and the likeness of God* (Gen. 1:26-27), and at the same time an excellent orator and writer. In the words of Bishop Atanasije (Jevtić), Mardarije "worked a lot and accomplished much, but he also suffered many bitter things at the hands of the Serbian Church Diaspora. This seems to be the inevitable fate of all missionaries and apostolic workers."[19] Bishop Mardarije was undoubtedly a martyr of conscience until the last day of his short earthly life (he reposed in the Lord at the age of 46). He built himself into a firm foundation for the acquisition of the foretaste of eternity and eternal knowledge among the Orthodox Serbs in America and Canada, or rather, among all Orthodox people in America and Canada.

In Philadelphia in 1917 he was raised to the highest monastic rank—the rank of archimandrite. The Russian Bishop of Aleutian Islands and North America, Alexander, recommended him to the North American diocesan council as the best pastor to oversee his flock in America and Canada (the name archimandrite is a compound word coming from the Greek *archi*, which means first or above, and the Egyptian word *mandra*, which means flock) and also a man "well-known in Russia, undoubtedly energetic, and as far as I know him from the brief time that I have known him, a talented man and a knowledgeable psychologist of his own people."[20] Already from January 7th to 9th, 1918, Mardarije stayed in Lackawanna, New York, where he consecrated the Church of Holy Archdeacon Stephen,[21] and in the same year he became parish priest of the Holy Resurrection Church in Chicago, Illinois.[22]

---

[19] Bishop Atanasije, *Contemporary Ecclesiological Reminder on the Diaspora*, pp. 14-15.

[20] *American Srbobran*, November 3, 1917, in Dragutinović, p. 36.

[21] *Memorial Book*, Saint Sava Monastery, Libertyville, Illinois, 1953, p. 363.

[22] "1918—Reverend Mardarije becomes parish priest at Holy Resurrection," (http://serbiancathedral.org/information/parish-info/cathedral-timeline).

During 1919 Archimandrite Mardarije lived in the Russian emigrant home at 347 East 14th Street in New York City. At the All-Russian Assembly in 1919 in Cleveland, Ohio, which was held under the dark shadow of political developments in Russia, Archimandrite Mardarije was chosen to be the bishop "for the conduct of business of the Serbian Church under the Russian Church jurisdiction."[23] But being well aware of the seven Ecumenical Councils and their canons, he did not wish to be consecrated without the agreement of the Serbian Orthodox Church. Mardarije never, as a monk or later as a bishop, strayed from the sacred canons of the Orthodox Church. The place, or rather the role, of a bishop, and the manner of his election (τόπος καὶ τύπος—*topos kai typos*, Greek) were well known to him even from the student days in Russia.

Bishop Mardarije in 1930.

And still this election was not without consequences that would come from Belgrade. Upon his arrival in America, Archimandrite Mardarije set as his first task a solution for the organization and unity of the Serbian clergy in America. Upon his election to the episcopate by the Russian Orthodox Church, he wrote to his Serbian priests in Pittsburgh:

> When it was suggested to me by the Russian Church that I assume the duty of the head of the Serbian Church in America, I set some conditions to the Russian Church, and the main condition was that our Serbian Church in America be independent. This condition of mine was fulfilled. So far, for all of the disorder and chaos in our churches, we had an opportunity to blame

---

[23] Dragutinović, p. 33.

Archimandrite Mardarije (Uskoković), the superior of Rakovica Monastery and the principal of the Monastic School, with the faculty and students (1920–23).

the Russians, but from now on the fate of our Church is completely in our hands.... To the future council of clergy and laity I will hand over all of the authority granted to me by Russia, so that the council or anybody else can never think that I was fighting for authority at the time, when in fact my only goal was to see our Church independent and in order, even if I myself were only a janitor in it.[24]

"In the spring of 1921, by the decision of the Holy Hierarchical Assembly, Nikolai, the Bishop of Ohrid at the time, came to America and informed the Russian Metropolitan that he was assuming Church authority over the Serbs of America and Canada. He, with one letter, which is kept in the archive of the monastery, placed Archimandrite Mardarije as his deputy and made it Mardarije's duty to create a diocesan center and to found a monastery. But the idea of founding the Serbian monastery could not be realized at that moment."[25] In the period of 1921 to 1923 Archimandrite Mardarije

[24] Ibid., p. 34.
[25] Bishop Dionisije, "Kratka biografija Episkopa Mardarija" ("Short Biography of Bishop Mardarije"), *Memorial Book*, p. 61. In the same *Memorial Book* (p. 225), it is said that Mardarije served the last service in the old church in Chicago on Christmas of 1921, after which the church was closed.

was back in the homeland. He arrived in Belgrade in 1920 and he could not be consecrated since he had not been elected by the Holy Hierarchical Assembly of the Serbian Orthodox Church. Patriarch Dimitrije placed him as superior of Rakovica Monastery and the principal of the Monastic School at the same monastery. The time of his governing is remembered as successful and fruitful, despite the fact that the school was maintained without the financial contribution and help of the state.[26] His steadfastness in life and word was evident in the advice which he gave to the students of the Monastic School in Rakovica:

> Shine in your life as the candles shine in the church and burn as they burn before an icon so that people can see your life and your good deeds and through them glorify our Heavenly Father.[27]

During his three-year stay and work at Rakovica Monastery, Archimandrite Mardarije was active in many fields of ecclesiastical and societal work. He was invited to give a lecture in the hall of the Academy of Sciences, at the University, in gymnasia, at the Christian Community, at the Theological College, etc. He spoke on various topics, of which we will mention the following: "The Third Russia Which Is Coming," "The Destiny of Christianity," "Why the Slavic Idea Is Unattainable," "The Old Christianity and the New Age," "Russia and Slavistics," "The Woman in Christianity," etc.

There are many testimonies concerning the oratorical gift of Archimandrite Mardarije:

> At the podium he looked like a Byzantine fresco, spiritual, ascetic,[28] alive, picturesque, full of successful comparisons and inspired by a sincere feeling; he left a strong and unforgettable impression ... a learned orator.... The Society of Slavic Union prepared at the Hall of the Academy of Sciences an assembly, but the Hall of the Academy of Sciences was too small to receive

---

[26] We find out about this from a correspondence of Bishop Mardarije's relative (*Archive of the Serbian Orthodox Church in North and South America, Saint Sava Monastery in Libertyville, Illinois*)

[27] Dragutinović, p. 91.

[28] Jovan Dajković about Bishop Mardarije as an orator, *Pravoslavlje (Orthodoxy)*, September 15, 1979, in Dragutinović, p. 103.

all who had come—so many were turned away....[29] The orator was greeted enthusiastically and during his speech was interrupted by the applause of the impressed listeners.[30]

Archimandrite Mardarije asked the Holy Hierarchical Synod in Belgrade several times to appoint a bishop for America and Canada, and he cited several reasons for this. As the main reason he pointed out the distance from Belgrade as a real difficulty for the Orthodox Serbs in America. Based on these requests, the Holy Synod on October 18, 1922, appointed Bishop Nikolai (Velimirović) to be the administrator, which was the duty that up until then had been performed by Archimandrite Mardarije (Uskoković). At the request of Bishop Nikolai, the Synod of the Serbian Orthodox Church released him from the duty and on December 1, 1923, placed Archimandrite Mardarije as the administrator of the Serbian Diocese of America and Canada.[31] Furthermore, by the act of May 9, 1924, the Consistory of the Serbian Diocese of America and Canada asked the Holy Hierarchical Synod, or rather the president of the Holy Hierarchical Synod, Patriarch Dimitrije, to consecrate a bishop for America and Canada, expressing their desire that this should be Archimandrite Mardarije.

So at the beginning of 1923, Archimandrite Mardarije went to America in order to continue his difficult labors in the organization of the Serbian Orthodox Diocese of America and Canada, which he had, by divine providence, started earlier on the distant American continent. The letter of the Consul General of the Kingdom of Serbs, Croats, and Slovenes in Chicago addressed to the Ministry of Foreign Affairs and Faith, dated April 3, 1923, testifies that upon his return to America in the beginning of 1923, at a clergy conference, which he convened and which was held from February 8-21, 1923, in Gary, Indiana, Archimandrite Mardarije

> achieved that which to everyone had seemed impossible until then, which was to unite all of our clergy in the common work of the organizing of the Serbian Orthodox Church in America.

[29] Dragutinović, pp. 92–93.
[30] Ibid., p. 92.
[31] *Pismo Patrijarha Dimitrija (Letter of Patriarch Dimitrije)*, no. 3875, *Archive* of the Serbian Orthodox Church in North and South America.

Twenty-eight priests out of the twenty-nine that were in America recognized him as the leader of our Church. He organized the Diocesan Consistory [the president of which was Archimandrite Mardarije—ed.], started up the official diocesan bulletin called *The Serbian Church*, and examined all the questions referring to the inner organization of the Diocese and to the relations with the church-school communities.[32]

Even before that, on January 30, 1923, Mardarije sent reports from Chicago to all the clergy concerning his election as the administrator, adding: "In all of your services, aside from His Holiness our Patriarch Dimitrije, you ought to commemorate also His Grace Bishop Nikolai, whose canonical domain our diocese still falls under."[33] After the clergy conference was held, on March 5, 1923, Archimandrite Mardarije informed all the parishes that from then on all of the legal and ecclesiastical questions should be sent to the ecclesiastical court at the following address: Serbian Eastern Orthodox Diocese, 1905 Fowler Street, Chicago, Illinois.[34] His activities upon his arrival from Serbia involved the visiting of all the parishes and the consecration of the ground and the churches in Duluth, Minnesota,[35] Farrell, Pennsylvania, etc.[36] (Patriarch Dimitrije in one of his letters asked Archimandrite Mardarije to inform him about the way that he was consecrating the newly built churches[37] and also informed him that he would send him the holy chrism and a

---

[32] Dragutinović, p. 41. "At this conference, the question of financial support for the bishop and the diocese was regulated. The clergy agreed that every one of them pay $5 a month to the Diocesan Fund, and the church community in Chicago took upon itself a responsibility to cover the diocesan administrator's apartment expenses." (Bishop Dionisije, "The Creation and Organization of the Serbian Orthodox Church in America and Canada," *Memorial Book*, p. 70).

[33] *Archive* of the Serbian Orthodox Church in North and South America.

[34] *Archive* of the Serbian Orthodox Church in North and South America.

[35] On September 30, 1923, in Duluth, Minnesota, he consecrated the foundation and gave blessing that the name of the future church be Saint George the Great Martyr (*Memorial Book*, Saint Sava Monastery in Libertyville, Illinois, 1953, p. 297).

[36] Saint George the Great Martyr Church was completed in 1924, and "it was consecrated in the same year by Archimandrite Mardarije, with the blessing of His Holiness Serbian Patriarch Dimitrije, at the time the Administrator of the Diocese of America and Canada" (*Memorial Book*, Saint Sava Monastery in Libertyville, Illinois, 1953, p. 302).

[37] *Letter* from October 23, 1924, *Archive* of the Serbian Orthodox Church in North and South America.

*Hieromonk Mardarije with clergy and laymen
in front of St. George Church in East Chicago (Indiana Harbor),
Indiana, 1924.*

The Chicago Bishop pictured arriving in New York aboard the Steamship "France"
after a tour of Serbia

certain number of antimensia, which testifies to the pastoral care of the Serbian patriarch so that everything would be *done decently and in order* (1 Cor. 14:40). In the letter to the Serbian Patriarch Dimitrije sent from Chicago on May 29, 1923, Mardarije characteristically says: "Having arrived in America by the will of God and the decision of Your Holiness and of the Holy Synod, in order to organize and administer the Serbian Diocese in this land, I have found a completely uncultivated field, a neglected field, in some places full of weeds and thorns. The merciful God helped me to organize this Diocese with my brethren."[38]

It is very important to mention that the God-pleasing life and the blessed work of Archimandrite Mardarije were met with a very good response not only from the Serbian people but "also from Americans, with whom he is in excellent relations."[39] "And aside from that, Mr. Mardarije holds lectures frequently at American universities, churches, and clubs about our nation and state, spreading excellently the propaganda which is to the benefit of our country."[40]

Božidar Purić, the Consul of the Kingdom of Serbs, Croats and Slovenes, said that Bishop Nikolai (Velimirović) gave a task to Archimandrite Mardarije before he departed Belgrade to "by any means necessary buy a property in the vicinity of Chicago where he will build a monastery dedicated to Saint Sava, a theological school and a printing press, an orphanage, and altogether the center of the Serbian religious life in America."

In 1923 Archimandrite Mardarije founded the Serbian Orthodox Diocese of America and Canada with its see in Chicago. That same year, in the beginning of August, he bought 33 acres of land in Libertyville, Illinois. Mardarije sought such a property as would be suitable for the needs of a monastery. North of Chicago he found a beautiful property with a winding river, the Des Plaines River, which

---

[38] *Letter*, Diocesan No. 55, *Archive* of the Serbian Orthodox Church in North and South America.

[39] The Consul General of the Kingdom of Serbs, Croats and Slovenes in Chicago, in the report from April 3, 1923, to the Ministry of Foreign Affairs and Faith, in Dragutinović, p. 41.

[40] The Consul General of the Kingdom of Serbs, Croats and Slovenes in New York, in the report from April 17, 1924, to the Ministry of Foreign Affairs and Faith, in Dragutinović, p. 42.

reminded him very much of the kind of land where monasteries in the homeland had been built.

The land for the monastery, orphanage, and the elderly home, as well as a certain section set aside for the cemetery, was consecrated on September 3, 1923. Divine Liturgy was served out in the field close to the Saint Sava Serbian Home, where he lived (Saint Sava Serbian Home had been blessed one year before that).

> No one is ever going to dig over this cemetery and disturb the peace of our departed ones or desecrate either the sanctity of the graves or the due piety that our people have toward their departed ones. At the monastery there will always be a hieromonk who will regularly serve in the church and on certain days will do memorial services at the cemetery.[41]

At the beginning of 1932 the first Serbian grave was dug.

How much Bishop Mardarije had built himself into the foundation of the Diocese of America and Canada, for which he had built the center at the Saint Sava Monastery in Libertyville, Illinois, is to this day testified to by that very monastery in Libertyville, which also points out the obvious sacrifice which he made for its construction. All the circumstances were set against the very thought that such a thing might be possible. We will mention a few obstacles.

First, the disunity among the Serbs and the pain that Bishop Mardarije suffered because of it.

> It is hard for me to hear that Serbian brothers persecute each other and hate each other. My heart hurts and I suffer in my soul, and I am ready to lament this even today when one ought not to cry, when I see that brothers persecute each other and hate each other.[42]

In Mardarije's example we see how the martyric, ascetic ethos of a Christian, the ethos of sanctity, which had been developed

---

[41] Dragutinović, p. 84. It should be noted that Archimandrite Mardarije announced on his own that the consecration of the monastery grounds would be on September 3, yet he did inform the Serbian patriarch about this in a timely manner (*Letter* from May 29, 1923, Diocesan No. 55, *Archive* of the Serbian Orthodox Church in North and South America). He added to this: "I was hoping that Bishop Nikolai [of Ohrid—ed.] would come in May and do it himself, but there are no signals of his coming soon."

[42] Dragutinović, p. 56.

throughout the two millennia in the Church, was the inspiration for the "community of the Saints," but at the same time it was a "stumbling block" to the so-called "common sense" of the secularized Serbs, who in their resistance toward the holy bishop only revealed the egotistical emptiness of their being removed from Christ. There were some even among the clergy who did more harm than good.

Mardarije's attitude toward his persecutors and slanderers was the best testimony of his authentically Christ-like being. Through his relations with his enemies we are reminded of the commandments of the Lord and of the path toward being filled with the Holy Spirit here and now. Dr. Božidar Purić said of Bishop Mardarije that he was a man ready

> to be an example through the renouncing of everything, and first of all the renouncing of his very self.... He was a monk without hypocrisy, without one grain of envy or hatred, without any vanity. Understanding and forgiveness were not a problem for him because he was goodness without passion... Physically beautiful, lively in his motion, unreal like a dream.

Father Dragutinović also adds that "his voice was Christ-like and meek, soft and pleasant; his vocabulary very rich and diverse, his thought crystal clear."[43] At the insolent accusations of some individuals about the supposed misappropriation of resources, he smiled with sadness and within himself whispered a prayer, "Father, forgive them, for they do not know what they do."[44]

Abbot Nikodim (Stojaković) in his farewell speech by the tomb of Bishop Mardarije said among other things:

> We priests hindered him and stood in the path of his work. We oftentimes aggravated him and wounded him in his heart, but he took no revenge for any of this. He prayed to God to forgive us and to enlighten us because we know not what we do. When the priests offended him most deeply, he never fought back, but would close himself in his cell and cry bitterly. It is obvious that

---

[43] Dr. Božidar Purić, *Biography of Božidar Ranković* (1963), p. 176. Both quotations in Dragutinović, p. 21.
[44] Dragutinović, p. 64.

he had no thought of revenge, because on his death bed he pro-
moted some of you priests into the rank of protopresbyter and
some others with a red sash.[45]

The next thing that we should mention is the lack of monetary
resources even for the most basic needs of Archimandrite Mardarije, who was not infrequently in the position to literally starve.
Božidar Purić, in his book *Biography of Božidar Ranković*, quotes
the following:

> Whenever I would object to him not securing a bigger sum for
> the beginning of the construction, he would say: 'Don't worry,
> Božice [a diminutive, endearing nickname for Božidar—trans.].
> People will give as soon as they see the foundation....' 'Mardari-
> je, you will become Darmarije [meaning "trouble maker;" word
> play—trans.],' I would rebuke him jokingly, to which his usual
> response would come: 'Božice, if we could only get up to the
> roof, people will give. The Serbian people are good....' But be-
> fore the roof was set, there was a meeting in Chicago, which
> asked of him to present the books to them, barely stopping
> short of accusing him of theft. Appalled and in disbelief that
> such a thing was even possible, Mardarije could not even open
> his mouth.[46]

Third, he suffered from the heavy illness of consumption [tu-
berculosis of the lungs—trans.], about which the Consul General
of the Kingdom of Yugoslavia Vukmirović wrote characteristic and
existentially moving words that Bishop Mardarije "had to fight off
death day by day in order to dedicate each day to working with our
people... He considered himself God's priest of peace and love."[47]

Fourth, a world crisis was on the horizon, a crisis that could
have realistically stopped the construction of a grand monastery.
Not infrequently, Mardarije made payments for the land from his
more-than-modest income, so that the people soon started saying,
"Mardarije is building a monastery while starving to death." A poet
describes his ascetic persona in the following way:

[45] "Ujedinjeno Srpstvo" (United Serbs), Chicago, Dec. 25, 1935, Dragutinović, p. 147.
[46] Dragutinović, p. 63.
[47] *American Srbobran*, December 19, 1935, Dragutinović, p. 147.

An ascetic living off of bread and salt,
Doing for his brethren what is acceptable to heaven,
And constructing a temple to the God of Saint Sava,
He was building himself into it.[48]

He planted fruit trees on the property by himself, and his two hands arranged rose bushes and stone-paving blocks around the property. Dragutinović wrote:

> In the days when he stayed in Libertyville he would rise at dawn and go to the construction site and, together with the workers, with great physical struggle, he would work on the scaffolding around the rising structure of the church, which from day to day showed more and more of the beautiful and harmonious lines, and this image gave him strength so that he would persevere, so that he would not languish until he saw the end of this labor and the Serbian people within it. When he was not working on the construction, he was planting various trees around the monastery property, flattening the existing paths and building new ones, and digging draining ditches.[49]

The Holy Hierarchical Assembly elected Archimandrite Mardarije to be the bishop on December 7, 1925. His health was already deteriorating then and he was intending, on the advice of doctors, to set out on a journey across the Atlantic by boat to go to Belgrade in the middle of May of 1926, after his intended recovery in Arizona, where he was supposed to "restore his health out in the sun and silence for the great and exhausting trip to Belgrade and back." His recovery time in Arizona was much shorter than would have been required by his condition at the time. Because of the invitations that were arriving from Belgrade, he decided to set out earlier. He wrote about this on March 26, 1926, to his friend of many years, Luka Grković:

> From Belgrade they advised me that nobody should come with me to the consecration.... I personally do not need anyone, but some people have not even thought about the fact that an event as important for the Serbian people in America as the consecra-

---

[48] Dragutinović, p. 157.
[49] Ibid., p. 61.

tion of the first Serbian bishop in America should be performed in as festive way as possible. Puny souls, little people. I want to return from Serbia to America as soon as possible and to begin as a bishop my hard and holy work, in which, I firmly believe, all those who are honorable and honest in America will help me. Until now, I myself have found it hard to believe how many friends I have among our people in America.

But still he went to Belgrade in April by himself, even though in the *Herald* of the Serbian Diocesan Fund in America, written after the election of Archimandrite Mardarije for episcopate, it was said that the consecration would be attended by a delegation for the following reason:

> In order to show everyone in our dear fatherland that our diocese is a daughter of the Serbian Church, we want our new bishop to receive his consecration and his authority in Belgrade at the hand of the Serbian patriarch.... And with our bishop there should be a delegation which will represent our emigration properly in the fatherland, before both the spiritual and worldly authorities.[50]

In any case, on the eve of Palm Sunday, Mardarije's nomination was declared, and the day after, on the very feast day of Palm Sunday, April 25, 1926, his consecration was performed festively in the Cathedral Church in Belgrade, the capital city of the Kingdom. The Serbian diocese in America and Canada, which had existed since 1921, received its own first bishop.

The next day, by the decree of Patriarch Dimitrije and by the order of the king, he was appointed the bishop of the Serbian Orthodox Diocese of America and Canada. He was 36. About his consecration, the Belgrade newspaper *Politika* on April 26, 1926, wrote:

> The consecration of His Grace Mardarije, our first Bishop of America and Canada, started a little before nine o'clock, yesterday in the Cathedral Church. The service was conducted by the Patriarch Dimitrije, the Bishop of Dalmatia and Istria Danilo, and the Bishop of Strumica and Tetovo Serafim.[51]

[50] Ibid., p. 48.
[51] Ibid., p. 53.

The *American Srbobran* of July 1, 1926, wrote about his return, now as Bishop Mardarije, to New York, on June 13, on the boat *France*. The same newspaper informed on July 17 that on Tuesday evening, June 13, the first bishop of the Serbian Orthodox Church in America and Canada, Mardarije (Uskoković), had arrived in New York, as well as that on that occasion the Serbian colony in New York prepared a magnificent welcome for him.[52] On the shore, a countless multitude of Serbs met him, led by Mihailo Pupin.[53] In all the speeches that were made on that occasion the importance of having a permanent head of the Serbian Orthodox people and their future generations in America and Canada was accented the most. The joy was all the greater because that first bishop was Mardarije Uskoković.

D. Dragutinović describes the mood or rather the astonishment of people at the moment of Bishop Mardarije's arrival when they saw him:

> They expected a despot but they saw a lamb of God. What an evangelical pastor, what a servant of God, what a guardian of the flock that was entrusted to him. The young servant of God was meek and full of humane goodness, ready for sacrifice and to renounce even himself, overfilled with love, and thirsty for the goodness of people. As such he stretched out his hands for an embrace and displayed his open heart to all of the American Serbs. In his gaze and in his countenance one could already see a mark of an earlier martyrdom, an image of life in Russia.[54]

Upon his arrival in New York, that same evening he telegraphed Patriarch Dimitrije (Pavlović) that he would soon travel from New York to Chicago. Upon returning to America Mardarije began his missionary work, his role as a confessor and a martyr, who cultivated an immeasurable love for his own people. He was raised on this

---

[52] Ibid., p. 94.

[53] Also known as Michael I. Pupin (1858–1935), Ph.D., LL.D. He was a renowned Serbian American scientist and inventor (34 patents in the fields of telecommunications, radiology, roentgenology and telegraphy), a professor at Columbia University in New York (two of his students won the Nobel Prize), a founding member of NACA in 1915 (which later became NASA), a Pulitzer Prize winner in 1924 for his autobiography, a philanthropist and patron of the arts, and devout Orthodox Christian.—Trans.

[54] Ibid., p. 63.

love as a child, listening from his earliest days to stories about the heroism and the chivalry of individuals among his people.

When he was placed at the head of the newly founded diocese, Bishop Mardarije, even though his health was poor, made great efforts to organize the diocese and set it in order. What kind of efforts these were and how many of them there were, we can see, among other things, from his numerous epistles, filled with quotes and explanations of the words from the Holy Scripture, as well as from his many visits to churches all over America and Canada. "I visited local churches one by one as each one invited me. The people everywhere were exhilarated to welcome their first bishop."[55] That very same year, 1926, Bishop Mardarije visited the Church of the Nativity of the Mother of God in Clairton, Pennsylvania, and at the same time ordained to the deaconate Andra Popović (who would later become a protopresbyter).[56] That same year, on December 19th, the bishop blessed the church and the hall of the Holy Great Martyr George in Oakland, California.[57] In 1927 the bishop consecrated the Serbian Home in Steelton, Pennsylvania, by the church of Saint Nicholas.[58]

The bishop's illness was very serious and at that time there was no cure for it. In spite of that, nothing could stop him from visiting, encouraging, and strengthening the people, first of all by his personal example and life. Concerning the bishop's illness, his physician, Dr. Mihailo Matanović (the bishop's classmate), states:

> Bishop Mardarije is here under my supervision. His treatment requires a long time, perfect rest, and absence of cares. If he stops in the near future with all of his travels and if he has rest and proper nutrition, there is hope for recovery...[59]

[55] Bishop Mardarije of America and Canada to Patriarch Dimitrije, Libertyville, Illinois, Confidential, September 5/18, 1926, in: Bishop Sava of Šumadija, *The History of the Serbian Orthodox Church in America and Canada 1891-1941*, Kragujevac: Kalenić, 1994, p. 208.

[56] *Memorial Book,* Saint Sava Monastery, Libertyville, Illinois, 1953, p. 261.

[57] *Memorial Book,* Saint Sava Monastery, Libertyville, Illinois, 1953, p. 447.

[58] *Memorial Book,* Saint Sava Monastery, Libertyville, Illinois, 1953, p. 496. The Executive Board members of the newly founded Holy Trinity Church in Rock Springs, Wyoming, in their letter from October 31, 1926, asked Bishop Mardarije to visit them. They received a positive answer that the visit would take place the following month (*Archive* of the Serbian Orthodox Church in North and South America, Saint Sava Monastery in Libertyville, Illinois).

[59] *American Srbobran*, March 15, 1927, in Dragutinović, p. 94.

> Against a categorical order of four doctors, Bishop Mardarije suddenly left for Chicago today. He needed to stay in Arizona the entire summer... I renounce any kind of responsibility for his departure for Chicago.[60]

His illness was also further aggravated by external circumstances, concerning which a chronicler writes the following:

> Even before 1927 the bishop was often ill, but that year the illness became a great threat and it was harder and harder, giving us all an impression that he was not going to live long. For the sake of healing and recovery he went several times to the soothing, blossoming, sunny South, to Arizona, where he would in a short time recover, only then to have the illness come back with more strength and as a greater threat. This would happen especially in those times when he would, due to matters that he had to attend to, leave Arizona for some time and travel to other parts of America in order to fulfill his duties within the diocese or for the monastery. Those matters, travels without rest, and especially discord among the people, prompted by unfounded malicious slander by some priests and a few Serbian academics, contributed to the bishop's illness spreading rapidly and reducing his physical powers, which were already thin, and announcing the end of his life.[61]

In June of 1927 Bishop Mardarije wrote to the Holy Hierarchical Synod about his visit to Los Angeles, where he managed to restore unity and to make peace among the local Serbs. Visiting the far West of the great country, he fell ill in the hospital in Los Angeles and stayed there for treatment for five weeks, after which he again went to Arizona, to Phoenix. Concerning his illness one guard at the monastery said:

> The late bishop was sick with tuberculosis. He had one lung removed and in its place was placed an artificial lung made out of cellulose or some such material. For this reason he needed a lot of air, so he slept out here on this terrace for the last three years and this is where he received visitors also.[62]

---

[60] *American Srbobran*, May 24, 1927.
[61] Dragutinović, p. 59.
[62] Ibid., p. 183.

The daily need for the numerous gifts of the first head of the Serbian people in America and Canada was huge. Faced with the problems of disunity and discord among some of the Serbian clergy, who stirred up the people and created divisions, this great man of prayer, who was pleasing to God and exemplary before his people, as a true child of his heavenly Father, raised his arms toward heaven just like the Psalmist, and cried out to the Lord with his voice:

> O Lord, why do those who afflict me multiply?
> Many are those who rise up against me...
> But Thou, O Lord, art my protector,
> My glory and the One who lifts up my head...
> Arise, O Lord, and save me, O my God! (from Psalm 3)

The diversity of the gifts or *charismas* of holiness in the Church is such that not one gift can say to another one, "I have no need of you" (cf. 1 Cor. 12:18-26). Bishop Mardarije lived this truth through the practice of church-people's assemblies. The first such church-people's assembly was held September 1–5, 1927, at the Saint Sava Monastery, in Libertyville, Illinois.

> According to the minutes, on the first day of the assembly, there were 100 delegates there, of whom 34 were delegates of the church-school communities, eleven of humanitarian organizations, 14 from the Serb National Federation, and also 4 delegates from other various organizations, 20 priests, and 13 members of the temporary Diocesan Council... Bishop Mardarije said that the draft of the constitution was written according to the template of the Church ordinances of the Metropolitanate of Karlovci, of the autonomous Church of Bosnia and Herzegovina, and according to the Church rules which are in effect in the Kingdom of Serbia, on top of which were added a couple of paragraphs which relate to the circumstances here.[63]

The troubles that Bishop Mardarije faced while he was ordering things in the diocese prompted him all the more to make it possible for the Diocese of America and Canada to obtain its own *Constitution* as soon as possible. Aside from everything stated above, he managed to put together a draft of the first constitution, which the Dio-

[63] Ibid., p. 68.

In front of the church of Saint Sava Monastery in Libertyville, Illinois, in 1934:
Priests Petar Stijačić and Pavle Marković, Bishop Mardarije,
Priests David Popović and Dušan Trbuhović.

cese of America and Canada soon after implemented, in 1927.[64] The
Constitution was accepted at the first and, consequently, historic
Serbian Church-People's Assembly. In the homily on this occasion
Bishop Mardarije said:

> The Lord gave me the fortune to live and to see today the open-
> ing of the Church-People's Assembly, the fruit of my and your
> work of many years and the guarantee that the life of the Ser-
> bian Church in America and Canada will be what it ought to
> be. It seems to me like everything is a dream. It seems to me like
> these are still some kind of negotiations and agreements, but
> actually we are facing reality. This is the Assembly which will
> solve our most important question in the Diaspora—the ques-
> tion of the Serbian Orthodox Diocese, in which everyone will

---

[64] Regarding the writing of this constitution, Bishop Sava of Šumadija rightly says the
following: "This first Constitution, which became a regulator of the Church and people's
life in America and Canada, would go through several changes and additions in the
following years. But to this day the spirit of Rescript, imposed upon the Serbian Orthodox
Church by the Austrian emperor Franz Josef, would be felt" (*The History of the Serbian
Orthodox Church in America and Canada 1891–1941*, Kragujevac: *Kalenić*, 1994, p. 230).

be put in their place, where they belong according to our moral and spiritual strength.[65]

Concerning this Assembly Bishop Mardarije wrote a letter to Patriarch Varnava in which he pointed out that "in the Diocese of America and Canada today we have 32 parishes with 23 parish priests."[66]

However, as the life of the diocese went on and the construction of the monastery proceeded, the health of the first bishop declined.

> The bishop's illness was spreading. He oftentimes served in unbearable circumstances under the heavy miter and golden vestments in small churches. He walked oftentimes in processions with liturgical fans, even during winter, down the long streets of the workers' neighborhoods, with his knees almost giving way, while the cold winds from the north were howling through the American valleys.

During the illness of Bishop Mardarije four churches were built: in St. Louis, Missouri, in Loraine, Ohio, in Jolliet, Illinois, and in Youngstown, Ohio. There is a testimony of Mr. Pajo Boljac that speaks about the Christmas of 1932, when Bishop Mardarije, in the absence of the priests and the people due to the terrible cold,

Bishop Mardarije visiting Montenegro with the Metropolitan of Montenegro (1920-1938) and later Serbian Patriarch (1938-1950) Gavrilo (Dožić).

---

[65] Dragutinović, pp. 67-68. It should be noted that the Serbian Patriarch Varnava in his letter to Minister P. Živković commended the work of Bishop Mardarije: "His Grace Bishop Mardarije so far has made a fine success in the church, national and educational fields" (Synod. Number 2496/1374, December 8, 1930).

[66] Bishop Sava of Šumadija, *The History*, p. 459.

The celebration of the feast day of Savina Monastery
(Herceg Novi, in the coastland of Montenegro),
the Dormition of the Most Holy Theotokos, in 1930.

served Liturgy in Chicago in the presence of the church warden and
only a few faithful.[67] As a martyr of conscience he could never allow
himself to not serve Divine Liturgy on the feast of the Nativity of
Christ, and he managed to make his way to the Church of the Holy
Resurrection in Chicago in these horrible winter conditions, God
only knows how.

Undoubtedly, the numerous visits all over the huge diocese,
which encompassed an entire continent, could not but ruin his already fragile health even more, about which, among other things,
Mihailo Pupin also writes in a letter:

> I am very sorry that Father Bishop is sick. But even though that
> news saddened me very much, it did not surprise me. When the
> bishop told me in November about his intent to travel through
> the Western colonies, I was appalled, because I could not believe
> that a man who was so physically weak could ever realize such
> an intention.[68]

[67] *American Srbobran*, January 16, 1932.
[68] Mihailo Pupin to Radoje Janković, Consul General of the Kingdom of Serbs, Croats
and Slovenes in Chicago, New York, March 23, 1927, in Bishop Sava of Šumadija, *The
History*, p. 212.

The words of Bishop Mardarije from his epistle on Pascha of 1927 (written in Phoenix, Arizona) explain the shock of Mihailo Pupin the best:

> Today, my dear spiritual children, I rejoice with you as your bishop. I rejoice with you even though I am physically sick, because I believe that there is no death, knowing that I will live even after that hour when I depart this earth... Among all the duties that a man can have, there is no greater duty of which I would like to remind you on this day of Resurrection, than the duty of love. That is a duty above all duties...[69]

How heavy his cross was is evident in his *19*[th] *Epistle,* written on Pascha 1934, in which he writes a year and a half before his death:

> Over the 17 years of my service to God and people in America, I patiently bore my cross. Sometimes it was easy, sometimes it was heavy, but today that cross is heavier than ever before. At one point in time I was full of ideals, wanting to serve you and leave you with something permanent. But today I am exhausted; my knees are giving way under the weight of that heavy cross. Your bishop now speaks to his flock all over America and from the depth of a soul he cries out: "People, brothers, is there anyone among you who will help me carry my heavy cross, or are your hearts so hardened that instead of helping you are even adding a burden to my weak back?"[70]

In writing about Mardarije's death, the priest Živojin Ristanović, who was very close to the bishop, speaks about the conditions and the methods of Mardarije's work:

> Things were not in order in the Diocese. Self-will and disobedience were on the rise. Parental and episcopal advice was not helping. There was a real danger of destruction and demolition of that which had been created with heavy toil. Bishop Mardarije avoided to an extreme any kind of drastic measures. In one case he refused to execute the order of the patriarch about the removal of one priest, because he was deeply convinced that that priest knew the way to repentance. That path was always left open to anyone by Bishop Mardarije. But in some cases, in the interest of the Church and peace among the people, there had

[69] Dragutinović, p. 56.
[70] Ibid., pp. 133–34.

to be reprimands. In those cases the people unanimously stood behind their bishop and condemned the anarchy and the self-will of the culprits. But this further shook up and worsened his health and expedited his end.[71]

The teaching and dogma of the Church about the Holy Trinity and her ethos was preached by Bishop Mardarije mostly through his authentic Christian life in the sign of the Cross, by being crucified for those around him. The truth that God is Love, he proved daily through sacrificing himself, showing thus the truth about being in the image and becoming according to the likeness of God. This was the path of thorns that was walked by this confessor of Christ in the first half of the 20th century.

✳

During his episcopate Bishop Mardarije visited Serbia several times but he always oversaw (Greek ἐπίσκοπος / *episkopos*—overseer) the life of the Church entrusted to him. Thus, around Pascha 1928 he was in Belgrade, but in his *10th Archpastoral Epistle*, written at Pascha 1928, he wrote the following to his flock in North America:

> Despite everything, your love has tied me to you, my flock, and I yearn to go back to you as soon as possible. "Do not believe everything you hear," I say to you using the apostolic words [cf. 1 John 4:1], do not believe the rumor that I will receive one of the dioceses here in the Kingdom of Serbs, Croats and Slovenes, of Yugoslavia, and that I will stay here [in Belgrade]... Know that I have no intention to go to any diocese in Europe, because I have been by God's will tied to the diocese in America and Canada, and know also that I am not thinking of any other position in our Church except the one that I have right now. The peak of my earthly longing is that I serve to my last day the Diocese of America and Canada, my dear Serbian people in the New World, whom I have grown to love so much over the past twelve years of my missionary work in America and with whom I have become spiritually close in both good and trying times...[72]

---

[71] Protopresbyter-stavrophor Živojin Ristanović, "Bishop Mardarije," in: *Memorial Book*—30 years of Saint Sava Monastery and 60 years of the Serbian Orthodox Church in America, Libertyville, Illinois, 1953, p. 53.

[72] *American Srbobran*, April 19, 1930, in Dragutinović, p. 97.

Bishop Mardarije in front of the Patriarchal Residence in Sremski Karlovci,
with a group of bishops (from left to right: Mitrofan of Braničevo, Vicar Bishop
Maksimilijan, Emilijan of Timok, Mihailo of Šabac, Kirilo of Boka Kotorska,
Danilo of Dalmatia, and Mardarije of America and Canada)

Bishop Mardarije deeply felt what his people in the motherland
felt. He experienced all the misfortunes that his people experienced
and he prayed to God with sadness and suffering. Dragutinović describes his reaction to the news about the flood:

> In 1926, when there was a flood in one part of the State of Serbs,
> Croats and Slovenes, and water overtook many regions, de-
> stroying many cattle and many human lives, and famine started,
> Bishop Mardarije submitted a letter dated July 4/17 of that year,
> in which he urged the Consul General in New York to immedi-
> ately organize committees for the collection of humanitarian
> aid, both from our compatriots and from Americans, and he
> said he would do everything he could to ensure the success of
> that operation among our people and among Americans.[73]

---

[73] Dragutinović, pp. 57–58. This care and responsible relation toward a decision of the
Holy Hierarchical Assembly is evident in his letter of October 16, 1929, in which he
delivered monetary help to the Bishop of Dalmatia and Istria, Danilo (*Archive* of the
Serbian Orthodox Church in North and South America, Saint Sava Monastery in
Libertyville, Illinois).

When he could not go to the Assembly, Mardarije informed the patriarch and entrusted one of the bishops with his vote.[74]

Staying in Belgrade in 1929 during the Hierarchical Assembly, Bishop Mardarije gave an interview on November 21 to the Belgrade paper *Pravda*, in which he said among other things:

> In America there are about 3 million Orthodox people, in the order of strength: Russians, Greeks, Serbs, Romanians, and others. There appear to be about 120,000 Serbs in America, scattered all over the vast expanse and in the sea of foreigners, which is why a Serb in America clings to his country, is closely tied to his tradition, his native language, and his ancestors' testaments...[75]

This love poured forth from him in his first episcopal homily:

> I will fulfill the promise that I gave to You, O God, in Your temple, before Your people, because I was there with them. I saw how the fiery sea of forges and factories burns their bodies. Their hands were blackened, but I was afraid to stretch out my hand to them. I was afraid that they would think that I was a gentleman of some kind. So far I was a brother to them and from now on I will be their father and pastor.[76]

Regarding these visits to Serbia and Serbian lands, Bishop Sava says that Mardarije, because of the difficult material position of his Diocese and for the sake of securing some support, had spent fifteen months in Serbia at one time, from October 1929 to February 1931 ("We spent 15 months in the motherland working for the interests of our diocese.")[77] It is well known that on June 6, 1930, the new Serbian Patriarch Varnava was led to the throne of the patriarchs of Peć,

---

[74] And so on October 29, 1928, he informs the Assembly through the Consul General Purić that he entrusts his vote with Patriarch Dimitrije, and in case of his absence to Metropolitan Gavrilo Dožić (*Archive* of the Serbian Orthodox Church in North and South America, Saint Sava Monastery in Libertyville, Illinois).

[75] Dragutinović, pp. 75–76.

[76] Ibid., pp. 54–55.

[77] Bishop Sava of Šumadija, *The History*, p. 423. In the book written on the 30th anniversary of the monastery (pp. 48–49), Milan Radaković from Milwaukee says that Bishop Mardarije in the summer of 1932 went to Belgrade to ask for some assistance from the Patriarchate. "The Bishop is in Belgrade, the Secretary is in Chicago, the Treasurer is in Milwaukee. Creditors keep sending bills and threatening us with court. What are we to do?... There is no help from anywhere" (Dragutinović, p. 70).

and the act of enthronement was performed by bishops Georgije (Letić) of Timişoara, Josif (Cvijović) of Bitola, and Mardarije of America and Canada, who in the patriarchal entourage visited Kosovo and Metohija on that occasion.

From an Act from the Ministry of Foreign Affairs, Number 9783 of August 16, 1931, we can see that the monastery was yet unfinished and that the bishop's illness was preventing more money from being spent for the construction and the maintenance of the monastery.

In the end the monastery church was consecrated on September 6, 1931, and the news of this spread around among other Orthodox people.[78] In the course of the next two days the Second Church-People's Assembly was held, where it was decided that these assemblies would be held every four years. The Assembly made some changes in the Constitution of the Diocese, elected new members of the Ecclesiastical Court, and the Saint Sava Monastery became a part of our heritage.

Bishop Mardarije built this monastery with great efforts. He was often seen moving bricks on the back of his bicycle. Dragutinović quotes the following:

> Dr. Božidar Purić, the Consul General of the State of Serbs, Croats and Slovenes in Chicago at the time, said to Mr. Svetislav Bilbija that on one occasion, when he came to the monastery, he saw Bishop Mardarije carrying on his shoulders the heavy stone plates used to pave the paths between the gate and the church. At the objection of Dr. Purić that he should not be doing such heavy work, Mardarije said to him that he was doing it in order to save some money by not paying laborers to do the same.[79]

[78] Thus, the Greek Archbishop Athenagoras wrote to Bishop Mardarije the following: "I am still moved with the recent imposing ceremony of the consecration of the Monastery of Your Grace. From all my heart I congratulate Your Grace for this wonderful achievement, which is an honor to the brotherly Serbian people in this country and which on the other hand will leave the name of Your Grace immortal to the Serbian as well as to the rest of the Orthodox Churches in America." At the end of this letter, the Greek Archbishop asked Bishop Mardarije to send him an appropriate article and photographs, which would be published in the Greek newspapers, and then he concluded: "Especially I wish one photograph of Your Grace for my office and one for the newspapers" (*Archive* of the Serbian Orthodox Church in North and South America, Saint Sava Monastery in Libertyville, Il.).

[79] Dragutinović, p. 61.

The construction of this monastery was also generously contributed to by Mihailo Pupin who, as is well known, offered precious help to his bishop in every aspect. Upon the bishop's return from a treatment in Arizona, "he produced a new charter for the monastery and the property on May 22, 1935, in order to secure this heritage for the Serbian people."

Regarding his relationship with the great Pupin, it is noteworthy that Bishop Mardarije was the one who informed a great number of people about the repose of Mihailo Pupin and his funeral service, which was to take place at Saint John Episcopal Cathedral in New York.[80]

✳

After the construction of Saint Sava Monastery, the main mission of the first Serbian bishop in America and Canada was now for the most part fulfilled. Bishop Mardarije had organized the diocese and raised the first Serbian monastery. Wherever he served he was at the Holy Liturgy in the place of Christ, surrounded by the faithful people in one place (ἐπὶ τό αὐτό), the people without whom he could not have done this work, and the people who without their bishop could not be the Church of Christ. Bishop Mardarije was, despite his very poor health throughout the most of his life, with God's help, until the very end of his life, "again and again" aware of the important place and role of the bishop in the overall life of the flock entrusted to him. In his own words we recognize the echo of the ancient ecclesiology:

> Everything depends on the bishop. Of course, the bishop ought not to be an overlord, but a true missionary to the people.[81]

When on December 1, 1932, the Day of Union was celebrated as a national holiday in Yugoslavia, the Bishop of America and Canada, Mardarije, was in Belgrade and served Divine Liturgy in the Cathedral church on that day. After the service Bishop Mardarije gave a notable homily, which made a great impression on those

---

[80] M. B. Petrović, Pupin in Serbian-American Life before the First World War," *Serbian Studies* 4 (1986–87), pp. 5–28.

[81] Archimandrite Mardarije, Letter to Dr. Paja Radosavljević, Chicago, April 3, 1924, in: Bishop Sava of Šumadija, *The History*, p. 156.

that were present. That Day of Union, December 1, 1932, as it was commemorated in Belgrade and the rest of the country, was written about by the Belgrade newspaper *Politika* on December 2, 1932. A good example of the gift for homiletics Bishop Mardarije had was exactly his speech given before the king on this national holiday, when he, after finishing Liturgy, said the following among other things:

"On one occasion, I travelled from the eastern part of America by train to the western part of America, toward the Pacific Ocean and I was passing through the Great Plains. The train was going 80 to 90 km/h [50 to 56 mph—trans.]. Having arrived in the western states, having passed through the mountains, much greater than our mountains are in Herzegovina or Montenegro, the train, in order to arrive to its final goal on the shores of the Pacific, kept moving with the same speed of 90 km/h. Throughout the numerous curves, some of which were very sharp, the entire train shook, the glass windows rattled, and the frightened passengers thought that the train would roll down into the abyss at any moment. But to their great surprise, the frightened passengers saw a ten-year-old boy sitting still and flipping through the pages of a book, not paying any attention to the shaking of the train. Having asked him why he was not afraid of the train jumping out of the tracks and falling down into the abyss, the boy, with naïve but strong faith, answered: 'Why should I be afraid, when my own father is driving this train!?'... And so all of us 14 million Yugoslavs should never be afraid regardless of how much tumult our train, which is the State of Yugoslavia, goes through, either through the plains or through the mountain passes, because at the head of that train of our Yugoslav State is our common parent, the father of all Yugoslavs, our beloved King Aleksandar..." After the three-times repeated, popular, booming shouts of '*Živeo!*' ('Long Live') had calmed down, His Royal Highness the King with Princess Olga and Prince Pavle came to the Bishop of America and kissed his hand. This was the first occasion on which King Aleksandar kissed the hand of a bishop. Otherwise, he only kissed the patriarch's hand.[82]

[82] Dragutinović, pp. 100-101.

Consecration of the church of Saint Sava Monastery in Libertyville, Illinois,
on September 6, 1931.

In 1929 Bishop Mardarije consecrated the grounds for Saint
Sava Church in Merrillville, Indiana. The construction of a new
church was triggered by a quickly growing membership.[83] In 1924,
Saint Mary's Serbian Orthodox Church in Clairton, Pennsylvania,
was consecrated.[84] In March of 1931 the Serbian Singing Federation was founded and the Branko Radičević Choir from Chicago
became its first member. Bishop Mardarije served his last Liturgy in
the chapel in which the parishioners of the Holy Resurrection
Church in Chicago worshiped. On January 1, 1933, the first significant event took place in the new church hall. An elderly parishioner,
Ivan Vučetić, led the first *kolo* dance [or *oro* dance, traditional folk
dance among Serbs and other Balkan peoples, in which a whole
community dances together forming a circle]. On March 26, the
iconostasis was blessed, and on Pascha Bishop Mardarije served
the first hierarchical Liturgy in the new church. On June 25, the
new Holy Resurrection Church was consecrated.[85]

We had already seen how Bishop Mardarije dealt with challeng-
es from the outside. From the inside, however, suffering from tuberculosis, Bishop Mardarije still lived in deprivation and poverty. The
Epistle to the Hebrews points out the idea that God Himself pun-
ishes people pedagogically for our own good so *that we may be partak-
ers of His holiness* (Heb. 12:10). Mardarije had renounced everything
just to contribute as much as he could to set in order the Church life

[83] http://www.usaserbs.net/states/m/indiana.html?start=2
[84] http://www.waymarking.com/waymarks/WM6WBQ_1924_St_Marys_Serbian_
Orthodox_Church_Clairton_Pennsylvania
[85] http://serbiancathedral.org/information/parish-info/cathedral-timeline

of all our people in America and to make possible for the monastery to be finished. His illness was his *thorn in the flesh* (2 Cor. 12:7).

In the crypt at the Saint Sava Monastery, where the remains of the Bishop Mardarije (Uskoković) are in repose, there are also words from his testament:

> This holy monastery, as a place of assembly for Serbs in America, and a common house of prayer, as an eternal house of God, I leave as a heritage to my dear Serbian people so that they can after my death keep it and improve it, and so that they can leave it to their offspring in this New World as a beautiful monument of their national and religious conscience, and so that everyone to eternity can know and see, here on the other side of the Atlantic Ocean, that far from their motherland there were Serbs here. For all those Serbian men and women who helped me during the 18 years of work in America and thus eased my heavy burdens of governing the Serbian Church here, I pray to God to reward them with His mercy, and as for me, I leave to them and their homes my episcopal blessing.

In the testament put together on July 29, 1935, Bishop Mardarije left the monastery to the love of Serbian people and to his heir he said that he ought to love and keep the monastery as much as he loved it and kept it and that every other future bishop should reside at the monastery of Saint Sava in Libertyville:

> To the new Serbian bishop who will, after my death, be appointed from Yugoslavia, I recommend and urge him that his residence be here at the Saint Sava Serbian Orthodox Monastery in Libertyville, and that he love this monastery as I loved it and improve it as I have improved it by my hand, as I planted every tree on the property by my own hand.[86]

Let us also state here that the first Serbian bishop in North America had very active cooperation with other Orthodox bishops and jurisdictions (Greek, Russian, Syrian/Antiochian,) and even with non-Orthodox.[87] This is testified to by the records of various visits

---

[86] Dragutinović, p. 150.

[87] Cf. Letter to the Episcopal bishop Anderson (June 8, Arizona), where we can see that Bishop Mardarije was his friend (*Archive* of the Serbian Orthodox Church in North and South America, Saint Sava Monastery in Libertyville, Illinois).

and also by his correspondence which is preserved in the Archive of Saint Sava Monastery in Libertyville. We should especially point out the correspondence with the Greek Archbishop Athenagoras, who wrote to the Serbian bishop on various occasions.[88] Aside from that, he also wrote to the American president and other officials.[89]

As an illustration of his attachment to the new homeland and his trust in the USA, we read in *Time* magazine (Monday, December 5, 1932), in the article entitled "JUGOSLAVIA: Patriarch for Prosperity":[90]

> "More than 1,000,000 Jugoslav emigrants in America are suffering on account of the Depression," said their Bishop Mardary in Belgrade last week to His Holiness Varnava Patriarch of the Serbian Orthodox Church. Straightway Patriarch Varnava commanded all Orthodox Jugoslavs in Jugoslavia to pray on the following Sunday "for the return of prosperity to the United States." Officiating in Belgrade Cathedral, Bishop Mardary voiced his joy at the Patriarch's prompt action, and declared: "Jugoslavs firmly believe that the United States is destined to play a high, historic role in consolidating the disrupted relations of mankind."

※

[88] There are a number of such letters. See the letter which Greek Archbishop Athenagoras sent to him on March 19, 1935, along with an updated list of Greek parishes in America (*Archive* of the Serbian Orthodox Church in North and South America, Saint Sava Monastery in Libertyville, Illinois). In the letter on February 15, 1932 (*Archive*), the Archbishop was deeply concerned for the health of Bishop Mardarije ("I am anxious to learn about your health. Will you, therefore, please let me know how are you feeling now?"). In this letter Athenagoras is requesting a copy of the Constitution and the Rules of the Serbian Orthodox Church in America, insisting not to be misunderstood, recalling their previous mutual agreement ("I want this information solely for the purpose of better cooperation between our Churches, in the spirit in which we talked together in Chicago").

[89] In response to Mardarije's letter of August 30, 1923, the secretary of the American president wrote already on the following day: "My dear Archbishop Mardary, the President has asked me to thank you cordially for your telegram of August 30th. He greatly appreciates this evidence of good will." One letter came from the former president Woodrow Wilson: "I deeply appreciate your kind and friendly message and beg to express again my very deep interest in everything that concerns the welfare of the Serbian nation." (Both letters are in the *Archive* of the Serbian Orthodox Church in North and South America, Saint Sava Monastery in Libertyville, Illinois).

[90] http://content.time.com/time/magazine/article/0,9171,882437,00.html

The Founder's Composition,
on the wall in the narthex of Saint Sava Church in Libertyville, Illinois
(by Miloje Milinković).

It is time that we make a note in this hagiography of the traces of the written works of Bishop Mardarije himself. It is clear to the reader that the circumstances of Bishop Mardarije's life did not allow for much literary activity even though this bishop sent around numerous letters.[91] Therefore we are going to talk only about his epistles right now. It was noted that the epistles "that he sent during his episcopal work in America and Canada were very deep in content, very heartfelt, and very educational, and as such they soothed the heart and soul of every Serb in America and Canada."[92] It is

[91] The newspaper *Sloboda* [*Freedom*] (no. 2, 1928, p. 5) published an article by Ž. Bunčić, in which it is said: "For a little more than three months I have been watching our Bishop, as he writes all day long in his bed, sick and despite the doctors' instructions. A basket of letters comes and goes every day.... Is it honorable to offend this man, who is willing to offer even the last bit of his strength on the altar of our common good? Is it right to make this man suffer, when he, serving even in his sickness God and people, burns out as a vigil lamp before an icon?"

[92] Dragutinović, p. 115.

enough to read his *17th, 18th and 21st Archpastoral Epistles* (see part 3 of this book), in order to see the apostolic and patristic character of Bishop Mardarije. One can also notice in them his spiritual kinship to Saint Sava of Serbia, whose words from his well-known *Sermon on the True Faith*—"The gracious God, ... according to the teaching and preaching of the Holy Apostles, elevates me to this Sainthood [=archiepiscopate], wanting through me 'to fill up what is lacking' [cf. Col 1:24]"[93]—ring out like bells from the homilies and the epistles of the hierarch Mardarije, who served and worked until the day that his illness took him. "His spiritual and intellectual strength were never in question even when he was very near death."[94] Aside from that we should point out his refined wakefulness and his sense of the existential anxieties, expectations and restlessness of men in the time that he belonged to.[95]

※

Bishop Mardarije did not have a chance to enjoy the fruits of his labor for very long. He reposed in the Lord on December 12, 1935, at 9:45 in the evening, in the 46th year of his life. He died in a hospital in Ann Arbor Michigan, writing his last Christmas epistle to his flock. A poet recorded it this way:

> He was great during his life,
> Even though his life was Golgotha,
> He was great on God's path that he treaded,
> Great in suffering and great in death.[96]

The bishop's friend and coworker of many years, priest Živojin Ristanović, left a written testimony about the bishop and the last days of his short life on earth and the moment when his soul was leaving his weak and tormented body.

> On December 10th of that year I was in Aliquippa, Pennsylvania, where on church business I stayed a few months. Around mid-

---

[93] Saint Sava delivered his *Sermon on the True Faith* in Žiča Monastery in 1220.
[94] Dragutinović, p. 75.
[95] In his letter to Patriarch Dimitrije (May 29, 1923, Diocesan Number 55, *Archive* of the Serbian Orthodox Church in North and South America, Saint Sava Monastery in Libertyville, Illinois) he said: "In America there is a revolution of spirits, constant incidents and unexpected surprises, mostly oriented against the spirit of Christ and His Church."
[96] Dragutinović, p. 157.

night the phone rang. They called from the hospital in Ann Arbor saying that Bishop Mardarije was on his deathbed and that he wanted to see me. The next day, December 11, at about 5 o'clock in the afternoon, I arrived at the hospital. The nurse led me to his room. Approaching the room, I heard his voice. I stood at the open door. The bishop was lying down on his back and was looking upward without blinking. As if he were talking to someone, he was saying a prayer out loud. I quietly entered the room and stopped. The bishop kept going, praying out loud, without pausing. That prayer was his own, unwritten and never read. He prayed in Serbian language, in order to switch to English, and then to Russian, and then back to Serbian. It is hard to write down that prayer in words just by my memory. I do recall couple of words though:

"Receive, O Heavenly Father, me, Thy servant, forgive me my sins. Have mercy on my people, my spiritual children. Keep them by Thy might, O Lord, bow down Thine ear and hear the cry of the orphans of my brother Stano (the bishop's brother died in a car accident in 1934 and left behind two children)... Have mercy on all of us - unworthy ones... Save and have mercy on the Serbian Orthodox people, on our Royal House, and all the Orthodox Christians. Forgive me, O God, as I do forgive everybody ... everybody. Amen."[97]

Finally, I decided to speak to him. I thought that he did not see me so I said: "Your Grace, do you see me? I came to visit you." But gazing onward in the same direction the bishop said: "I know you are here. I see you... I see you always, even when you are not with me... Thank you." And then he went on to repeat the same prayer. The nurse came and adjusted his pillow. The bishop only then looked around himself. I approached him and took a blessing. He started crying. His lips quivered, he wanted to say something. Tears started streaming down like a river out of his eyes. All of this lasted couple of seconds. And then on the bishop's face appeared an expression of heavy fatigue and exhaustion. His breathing was heavy. He gave a sign with his hand

[97] Protopresbyter-stavrophor Živojin Ristanović, "Bishop Mardarije," in *Memorial Book*—30 years of Saint Sava Monastery and 60 years of the Serbian Orthodox Church in America, Libertyville, Illinois, 1953, p. 55.

for the nurse to leave the room and then he pointed to the chair by the bed for me. I sat down and waited...

"Thank you for coming. See, I have made my peace with the Lord. I am ready. Pray for the repose of my soul."

He could not go on... Suddenly, he fell asleep like a man who just finished a heavy and exhausting trip... Finally, in the evening of December 12, he asked for some water. The nurse approached with a glass. The bishop looked at me and said quietly: "You, Father Žiko [endearing nickname—trans.], you give me the water." I took the glass of water from the nurse. She slowly lifted the bishop's head from the pillow. I gave him some water from a little spoon, one spoonful, and another... Then the bishop suddenly looked upward throwing his head back. Bishop Mardarije was no longer breathing. I looked at my watch. It was exactly 9:45 pm.[98]

Icon of Saint Mardarije, St. Sava Church in Jackson, California (by Miloje Milinković).

[98] Ž. Ristanović, "Bishop Mardarije," pp. 55, 57.

In the *American Srbobran* for December 13, 1935, there is the following telegram: "His Grace Bishop Mardarije, with words of love and blessing for his flock, Church and Fatherland released his saintly soul at 9:50 [pm], at the University Hospital in Ann Arbor, Michigan."[99]

Upon receiving the news of his repose, Patriarch Varnava with Archimandrite Vikentije and two deacons served the memorial service (parastas, panikhida) for Bishop Mardarije in the Patriarchal Chapel.

Bishop Mardarije was buried on December 18, 1935, at the Saint Sava Monastery in Libertyville. Until the very last moment, the plans for his burial were unknown. At that time there were no diocesan committees or lay committees for funerals. At the Saint Sava Monastery around two hundred people gathered. The Liturgy, funeral and burial services lasted for about four hours.

The body of Mardarije of blessed repose was now in a casket made of fir wood, with the writing, "+Bishop Mardarije 1889–1935." The body was dressed in full hierarchical vestments by the priests Sergei Snegiev, Petar Stijačić and Živojin Ristanović. In the middle of the church was set a bier for the casket with six big black candle stands with candles in them. Next to the casket was the analogion with the dikirion, trikirion and the bishop's service book, and at the center of his chest were the cross and the Gospel. Above his head was another analogion with the Gospel, which was read without ceasing by the priests, from the first memorial service on Saturday until the funeral on Wednesday. The church was open all the time and the people came to venerate the remains of their beloved bishop. The memorial services were held by the Greek bishop Kallistos (the emissary of Archbishop Athenagoras, whose message he read),[100] the Russian bishop Leontiy from Chicago, and the Romanian bishop Polycarp from Cleveland, and by priests from other

---

[99] Dragutinović, p. 143.

[100] In his telegram sent to the Diocese on December 13, Archbishop Athenagoras wrote: "I lament with all my soul the repose of my beloved brother Bishop Mardarije, who lived the life of a saint, dedicated to serving to our Orthodox Church" (*Archive* of the Serbian Orthodox Church in North and South America, Saint Sava Monastery in Libertyville, Illinois).

jurisdictions, accompanied also by the Consul Vukmirović for the Kingdom of Yugoslavia, Luka Hristiforović for the Serb National Federation and Božo Martinović for the Diocesan Council.

At the time of communion at the Memorial Liturgy that was served, the priest Ristanović read the testament along with the bishop's last will that on the day of his burial eleven priests be elevated to the rank of protopresbyter and four priests to be awarded with a red sash (among them were those who had given the bishop the most headaches, and this act only testifies to his Christian greatness).

After Liturgy at the Cathedral Church in Chicago, the casket was on its way to Saint Sava Monastery in Libertyville, where the body was displayed until Wednesday, December 18 in the morning, when Liturgy and the funeral service were conducted. People came from all sides, mostly from Chicago, Gary, South Chicago, Milwaukee, Joliet, Waukegan and other places. There were three bishops, Russian—Leontiy, Greek—Kallistos, and Romanian—Polycarp; 18 Serbian priests, 8 Russian priests, 2 Greek priests, and 2 Romanian priests. There were also 2 Episcopal priests present.[101] There were 7 Serbian priests who provided legitimate reasons for their absences.

The Liturgy at the monastery church was celebrated by the Russian bishop Leontiy, with all the other bishops and priests serving with him. Also in attendance were Consul Vlada Vukmirović from the Kingdom of Yugoslavia, the royal emissary in Washington Konstantin Fotić, who laid a wreath on the bishop's grave, the treasurer Luka Hristiforović of the Serbian National Federation, and Božo Martinović from the Diocesan Council. At the funeral, the casket was carried three times around the monastery, after which Bishop Leontiy, according to the testament of Bishop Mardarije, elevated the above-mentioned priests. Then the casket was lowered into the crypt in the monastery church, which had been prepared by Bishop Mardarije during his life. The last "Memory Eternal" was sung. Sorrowfully and powerfully it echoed through the church that was still missing the iconostasis (even though during the bishop's life

---

[101] The Bishop's Deputy, Živojin Ristanović, expressed gratitude to all of them individually with thank-you letters (*Archive*).

the icons were made by the well-known Serbian academic painter Uroš Predić from Belgrade).[102] As a poet wrote,

> All who hated him publically and secretly
> Were crying by his tomb remorsefully,
> And his deeds stayed as a testimony to
> How one should fight for the Church and his people.[103]

Bishop Mardarije was and remained a pauper. For this reason the Kingdom of Yugoslavia paid for the expenses for the burial of the first bishop of America and Canada.[104]

Upon the death of Bishop Mardarije, the Holy Synod named an administrator of the Diocese, Bishop Irinej of Dalmatia, until the election of the new bishop. Bishop Irinej administered from June 10, 1936, until the spring of 1938, when Bishop Damaskin (Grdanički) was elected to be the regular bishop for America and Canada, who had been until then the Bishop of Mukachevo-Prashev [at the time in Czechoslovakia—trans.]. He took over the duty of diocesan bishop on July 1 of the same year (and stayed the Bishop of America and Canada only until 1939).[105]

Approaching the end of this hagiography, let us quote the words of Božidar Purić, who wrote:

> The mission of the first bishop was done. He constructed the monastery and set the diocese on its feet. He did not enjoy the fruits of his labor for long. His illness in the dungeon of life was short lived. It was marked ahead of time because tuberculosis started tormenting him. Too often he served in unendurable summer heat, in the sweat of his brow, under the heavy miter

---

[102] Dragutinović, pp. 146–47.

[103] Ibid., p. 157.

[104] The newspaper *Ujedinjeno Srpstvo* from Chicago wrote on December 25, 1935, about Mardarije's funeral: "Looking at the small procession, we who are Serbian feel embarrassed. We are embarrassed before the folks from other nations and 5 to 6 policemen in front of our church. At the head of the procession there is the car carrying three wreaths: from Prince Pavle [Karađorđević, Regent of the Kingdom of Yugoslavia during the minority of King Petar II—trans.], from emissary Fotić and the Serb National Federation. Behind the first car there is the car with the casket, then two funeral homes' limousines with the Russian bishop Leontiy and five priests, followed by 8 (literally eight) automobiles with Serbian folks in the bishop's funeral procession" (Dr. Đoko Slijepčević, *The History of the Serbian Orthodox Church*, Volume 3, Köln/Cologne, 1986, p. 398).

[105] Bishop Dionisije, "The Creation and Organization of the Serbian Orthodox Church in America and Canada," *Memorial Book*, p. 73.

Icon of Saint Mardarije, Holy Assumption Church
in Sacramento, California
(by Miloje Milinković).

and golden vestments, in small churches with not much air. Too
often he would walk in winter in a procession, with liturgical
fans, down the long streets of workers' neighborhoods, with his
knees giving way, while the cold winds from the north were
howling through the American valleys.[106]

The life of Bishop Mardarije of blessed memory, which was pre-
sented here in a short format, actually has a wide importance for the
Church and the people. In speaking about him, the Athonite elder
Vasileios (Gontikakis) of Iveron said:

The Orthodox assembly and gathering have a concrete meaning
because there we see children rushing to receive communion

[106] See in: Dr. Đoko Slijepčević, *The History of the Serbian Orthodox Church*, vol. 3,
Köln/Cologne, 1986, p. 397.

Reconciliation of the Serbian clergy in America and Canada,
May 12–13, 1931, Youngstown, Ohio.

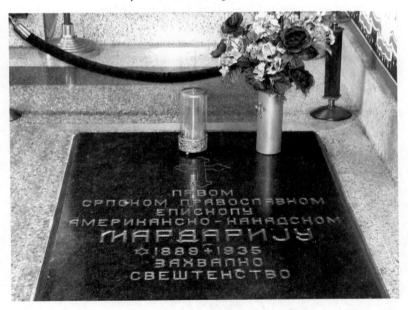

The grave of Bishop Mardarije, south side of the church of Saint Sava Monastery
in Libertyville, Illinois.

but at the same time we have with us those great spiritual figures who give us comfort, such as Abba Isaac the Syrian and the much tormented Bishop Mardarije.[107]

※

So the meaning of Bishop Mardarije goes beyond the narrow national framework. What a poet wrote about this worker in God's field is true:

> The Monastery and the first Serbian Diocese,
> To the honor and pride of all the future generations,
> Were left like two jewels to the Serbs,
> So that through them God's name could always be glorified.[108]

Still it is true that his ecclesiastical testament is handed down to all of Orthodoxy.

> An organizer of fantastic capabilities ... a civilian administrator and a spiritual leader for whom a Jew and a Christian were equally men of God, a man who endured countless attacks without wavering, who remained silent in the face of slander, and who stayed on the path of God; a monk who was also called a "social worker," a dreamer who dreamt of "the joyous moment of union of all the brotherly Slavic peoples around Russia into one common state," he was surely one of the most significant personas of the time. Picking one significant characteristic of his from among so many others is not an easy task.[109]

Our Faith without the saints—those from the past, the present, and the future—is just a secular ideology, brought down to the level of the world. This is why the numerous testimonies of the sacred image and life of Bishop Mardarije are so precious. His ascetic look and piercing gaze left an impression that one remembered for life, and almost all who wrote about him used the adjectives *holy*, *saintly*, and the like, when they described him as a man. "Everything is in his eyes," said Metropolitan Amfilohije [of Mon-

---

[107] Elder Vasilios said this during the Diocesan Days of the Serbian Orthodox Diocese of Western America in Los Angeles, California, in 2011. It was published in his book *The Thunderbolt of Ever-Living Fire* (Los Angeles: Sebastian Press, 2014), p. 141.

[108] Dragutinović, 157.

[109] *Savremenik (Contemporary) Magazine*, Number 13, p. 85, Paris, France.

tenegro and the Coastlands].[110] Đoko Slijepčević gave a very impressive description:

> A lively spirit, a wakeful conscience, unbreakable energies, determined for Slavic panhumanity—Bishop Mardarije Uskoković was an unusual man, who persevered in his time, among his people, and despite deep poverty. In his saintly life he was a martyr, who, as Jovan Bratić said, "created opportunities, and people to whom such a thing is given always stand far above average people, for whom the circumstances, or rather misfortunes, are always too great. And here is a reason for us to thank God that He gave us such a hierarch in those times, and it is not the first time in the history of our Church and people that the Almighty One has surprised us with people greater than anything that stood in their path."[111]

Knowing oneself and the ultimate purpose of one's life through the Christ-like life and work of Bishop Mardarije does not limit one to the area of the North American continent. Many pages could be written about the universal significance of Bishop Mardarije *for the life of the world* (John 6:51). This is the case for all true saints of God.

Bishop Mardarije left his sacrifice as a heritage not only to the East but also to the West ("that good thing which was committed to you," 2 Tim. 1:14), and even to the Muslims. Let us mention the testimony of a Muslim man who discovered Christ. His transformation and turning to the Lord led him to the Roman Catholic Church, whose member he remains to this day. His sincere conversion to Christianity and a real feeling of the presence of Christ the Savior was not achieved in the church where he attends Sunday services. This man in the last seven or eight years comes to pray at the Saint Sava Monastery in Libertyville, sometimes every day, at Matins and Vespers. He has not intended to leave the Roman Catholic Church after making such a step toward Christ, but the contributions which he had been giving to that church have been redirected to the Saint Sava Monastery. This man always prays by the tomb of Bishop Mardarije. He goes directly to the place where the earthly remains

---

[110] From Metropolitan Amfilohije's sermon on Bishop Mardarije, given at Saint Sava Monastery in Libertyville, Illinois, in December 2013.

[111] Quoted according to Dragutinović, p. 180.

of our dear bishop are buried. When asked why he stands right there, he said:

> When I pray at the Saint Sava Monastery, I like to stand by the grave of Bishop Mardarije. The peace and energy which I feel there calm down my mind and my thoughts, and at the same time even my shoulders and my neck are relaxed... In keeping company with Bishop Mardarije to the glory of God, I pray for the salvation of my 81-year-old father and my younger brother... It is easy for me to pray here and this can also help them to hear Christ's calling in their hearts.[112]

This short hagiography of Bishop Mardarije seems to always point to the lives of the Apostolic Fathers, the immediate disciples and successors of the Apostles. Briefly, the most obvious resemblance to the Apostolic Fathers is in the following.

First, the time when Bishop Mardarije lived and worked was a fateful time, a time of crisis (Greek κρίσις—judgement, decision, determination), for the life of the Serbian Orthodox Church in America and Canada, both from the temptations in the "Promised Land" and the inner problems (and even a few parasynagogues), as well as because of the fact that until the installation of Bishop Mardarije the faithful did not have a strong pillar in episcopal activity, the very extension of the work of Christ on earth through His Body—"the Church gathered around her bishop." The sacred work of salvation, which Bishop Mardarije of America and Canada performed in his role as a bishop and carried on his weak back, is exactly that "theanthropic apostolicity" of which Saint Justin (Popović) spoke. Having founded and organized the first Serbian diocese in America and Canada, just like the Apostolic Fathers did in their time, in circumstances which were not very promising, Bishop Mardarije—an example of a new man, an eschatological man in Christ—preserved the true faith of the Holy Fathers. He showed that the role and place of hierarchs is to be pillars in the very work of the extension of Christ's work on earth through His Body, which is the Church.

---

[112] R. Marić, *Holy Bishop Mardarije Uskoković*, p. 223.

Second, Bishop Mardarije succeeded in turning all of us into "one choir," one assembly (*sobor/sabor, synaxis*), which never parts ways (with one interruption from 1963-1991, when the schism happened). According to the words of Bishop Atanasije (Jevtić), "Only on a secondary level can we understand the Church as a group of scattered faithful people in a certain place or all over the world, but even then as faithful people they are not ultimately scattered, but they remain always called to the assembly that never parts ways."[113] Bishop Mardarije managed to achieve that through a proper ordering of his household, through the service which belongs only to the bishop, to God's host, who is responsible for presiding, overseeing, teaching, and being a judge. Bishop Mardarije showed through his meek attitude toward the weaker in faith, the ones who actually "do not know what they do," that the true power of Orthodoxy is in humbling oneself, even at the price of crucifixion, before those who are weaker.

Third, his relation toward the world that he lived in, beginning from the village of Kornet in the region of Lješani, through Serbia, Russia, and ultimately America was "for the life of the world." We would like to quote one example, when in the fall of 1914 a young man, a Jew, referred to him and asked him to help him in getting a job at the Trade Institute in Moscow. Mardarije helped him without any hesitation.[114] Aside from the testimonies delivered so far, for the sake of illustration, we will quote his words spoken at the First Church-People's Assembly, which took place between the 1st and 5th of September, 1927:

> Grant me, your bishop, the great joy that I be able, after the work and your decisions in this Assembly, to say to the Lord: Behold, O Lord, me and the children you gave to me, we are all saved![115]

We will conclude this short hagiography of Bishop Mardarije with the words of his fellow countryman, patriot, teacher and *gusle* player [a traditional Serbian folk instrument, which accompanies

---

[113] "Liturgical Life—the Core of Parochial Life," Atanasije Jevtić, *Theological Views*, Book 12, March 3, 1980, pp. 89–105, 92.

[114] *Blue Journal* (Russian magazine), no. 11, March 18, 1916, in Dragutinović, p. 5.

[115] Dragutinović, p. 67.

the singing of epic poetry—trans.], Petar Perunović, called Perun (from Pješivci by Nikšić, living at that time in Minnesota), who fought in the Balkan Wars and the First World War—words that convey the church-people's desires that our bishop had:

> Bishop Mardarije at first sight appears as a humble and meek monk of rather melancholic appearance. But underneath that monastic humility and meekness, like a spark within a rock, is a fiery revolutionary of a burning, sanguine temperament, capable of a great and lengthy battle. What torments were not suffered by that small and physically weak monk? One moment you see him as a fiery reporter, another moment as an apostolic missionary, another moment as a God-given orator and homilist, and in another moment as a very skilled organizer. In all these things Mardarije had nothing but success. Always modest, meek, and considerate, skillful and introspective, he tirelessly fought and marched forward."[116]

And Perun continues,

> People can say whatever they want, but they must admire him— how he lived with his miserable salary, and how he walked around in very poor clothing and a cloak in harsh winters to the consecrations of churches, and to inspire assemblies for the erections of churches. If any bishop of our day and age can be called a martyr, according to his struggles and battles for the Church, then Mardarije can be called a great martyr. If the Serbs in America care about work, order and peace in the Serbian Church in America, I believe that they will find in Mardarije not only a wise advisor and a good bishop, but also a true Christian, a fiery and progressive Serb and a brother, whose soul is full of love and sacrifice for our people in America.[117]

Mardarije's image is already present on the walls of the Orthodox churches in North America. Pious Orthodox people have already been looking at him only to recognize, understand, and resist the great temptations which stand in the path of the Orthodox, authentic, ascetic life in Christ. A common glorification by all the

---

[116] Dragutinović, p. 89.
[117] *American Srbobran*, April 7, 1926, in Dragutinović, p. 90.

people of Saint Mardarije of Libertyville, in the context of Divine Liturgy, meeting him permanently within the liturgical and prayerful Community of the Saints and church holidays in America and Canada, will be the first step on the path to a much clearer recognition of his patristic image, as a true parent of all the Orthodox Serbs. Even if they are not aware of it, he prayerfully watches over them and guides them as his family—he prays to God for all of us today more than ever before. Filled with the Holy Spirit during his life, he was a living saint, who walked together with our immigrants, our ancestors in the beginning of the 20th century. Many who perhaps do not even speak the Serbian language will find within their families the ancestors who had built themselves "as living stones," (1 Pet. 2:5) together with their first bishop, into everything that is of the Serbian Orthodox style and experience.

Prepared by
Bishop Maxim of Western America
and Presbytera Ružica Marić

* * *

Kontakion to Saint Mardarije of Libertyville,
Tone 8:

O tireless preacher of Christ the Lord,
Saint Sava-like leader of your people in the Diaspora,
Diligent builder and teacher of repentance,
[whose rule of life was: "Sowing Christian love,
spreading peace, quieting passions,
preaching good, and turning people into brothers."[118]]
O Saint Mardarije of Libertyville and America,
With all the Enlighteners of the American land,
Beseech the only Lover of mankind
To grant peace and unity to the Orthodox people!

[118] His own words became part of the kontakion to him, for they represent the life motto of Bishop Mardarije's work.

The Founder's Composition,
on the wall in the narthex of Saint Sava Church in Libertyville, Illinois
(by Miloje Milinković)

Synaxis of the Serbian Saints in America,
on the wall in the narthex of Saint Sava Church in Libertyville, Illinois
(by Miloje Milinković)

TELEPHONE: ASTORIA 8-1653

ΕΛΛΗΝΙΚΗ ΑΡΧΙΕΠΙΣΚΟΠΗ ΑΜΕΡΙΚΗΣ ΒΟΡΕΙΟΥ ΚΑΙ ΝΟΤΙΟΥ
GREEK ARCHDIOCESE OF NORTH AND SOUTH AMERICA
INCORPORATED

273 ELM STREET, ASTORIA, L. I.

NEW YORK   September 15   1931

To the Right Reverend Bishop Mardary,
Bishop of the Serbian Orthodox Church,
Libertyville, Ill.

My dear Brother-in-Christ:

   I am still moved with the recent imposing ceremony of the
consecration of the Monastery of your Grace. From all my heart
I congratulate your Grace for this wonderful achievement, which
is an honor to the brotherly Serbian people in this country
and which on the other hand will leave the name of your Grace
immortal to the Serbian as well as to the rest of Orthodox
Churches of America.

   Desiring to have an article appear in the Greek newspapers
in connection with this ceremony, I ask your Grace to please
send me a few notes regarding the building, etc., and also
some photographs. Especially I wish one photograph of
Your Grace for my office and one for the newspapers.

   Anticipating the pleasure to hear from Your Grace soon,
I am,

                              Yours cordially

                              Archbishop Athenagoras

                              of North and South America

The Letter of the Greek Archbishop Athenagoras to Bishop Mardarije

Orthodox Serbian Bishop
of Ohrid and America
December 11/24, 1922, Belgrade

Dear Father Archimandrite,

As His Holiness, the Patriarch, informed you, you are going to America in order to be the administrator for the Church there, until it is God's will that we come there.

Since neither the Church nor the Royal Government will pay you to fulfill this new duty, you are going to have to be supported by your parish, where you have served before. In regard to the extraordinary expenses concerning your travels and administration, you are going to talk to the clergy and the church communities about that.

Your first concern should be that our people be taught and directed to Christian life as our Orthodox Church has established. The pastoral and spiritual role of a priest has to be above any other role.

Pay special attention to those small colonies that do not have their own priests and arrange that neighboring priests visit them. In those colonies, however, where there are churches and priests, religious and educational activities have to be set on the right track.

All ecclesiastical legal issues which need to be examined by the bishop you are going to collect and send to us for consideration and resolution.

You will also make sure that in all of the property disputes and tribulations of some of our church-school communities you help them to fulfill their rights and secure their property.

We hope that our consular authorities, our clergy, and our people will meet you with the same trust that the Holy Synod has for you and we hope no less that you, with God's help, will justify our trust with your work.

May God be with you on your journey, both on water and on land (Is. 43:2-3) and may He help you in your service, which is full of labor but also full of dignity.

With God's blessing,
Orthodox Serbian Bishop of
Ohrid and America
Nikolai

TO MR. MARDARIJE USKOKOVIĆ, ARCHIMANDRITE

ство и наш народ предусрести Вас са оним истим поверењем, са

којим Вас Свети Синод шаље; а не мање се надамо, да ћете Ви, с

Божјом помоћу то поверење и радом оправдати.

Нека Вас Бог прати на Вашем путу, и на води и на суву

(Ис. 43, 2-3) и нека Вам Он помогне у Вашој служби, пуној

труда не пуној и достојанства.

С Божјим благословом

ПРАВОСЛАВНО-СРПСКИ
ЕПИСКОП ОХРИДСКИ И АМЕРИКАНСКИ

Николај

ГОСПОДИНУ МАРДАРИЈУ УСКОКОВИЋУ АРХИМАНДРИТУ.

A Letter of Saint Nikolai (Velimirović) to Saint Mardarije (Uskoković).

Поштарина плаћена у готову

Чековни рачун Број 53.002

ПОЛИТИКА

ВЛАДИСЛАВ РИБНИКАР, ОСНИВАЧ
рев. капетан, погинуо 1 септембар 1914 год.
ДАРКО РИБНИКАР, УРЕДНИК
рев. капетан, погинуо 21 септембар 1914 год.
Д-р СЛОБОДАН РИБНИКАР, ДИРЕКТОР
рев. потпоручник, умро 14 септембра 1924 год.
Директор: ВЛАДИСЛАВ СЛ. РИБНИКАР
Уредници:
МИОМИР МИЛЕНОВИЋ и ЈОВАН ТАНОВИЋ

ПРИМЕРАК 1 ДИН.
ТЕЛЕФОНИ Администрација 25-007
Уредништво: 25-010 и 25-005

Београд, среда 29 јун 1932
Број 8667 — Година XXIX.

ПРЕТПЛАТА ЗА ЈЕДАН МЕСЕЦ
За нашу земљу 20. За стране земље 45 дин.
РУКОПИСИ СЕ НЕ ВРАЋАЈУ.

ПОЛИТИКА
Поенкареова 31

Опште снижење каматне стопе и дисконтна политика Народне банке

I

Тешко стање наших исељеника у Америци

— Разговор са г. Мардаријем, епископом наших исељеника у Сједињеним Државама и Канади, који је прекјуче допутовао у Београд —

Епископ г. Мардарије

Убијен фашиста у Луксембургу

Рим, 28 јуна

Верски сукоби у Ирској

Даблин, 28 јуна

Како изгледа криза у Америци

— Разговор са православним епископом наших исељеника у Сједињеним Државама и Канади г. Мардаријем, који је допутовао из Америке —

ПОЛИТИКА

Демонстрације гладних у Чикагу

Владика Т. К. Алгуњски

Педесет година четничке
зада војводе Тодора
Алгуњског

Бујановац, 1 јула

Да ли је у америчкој провинцији сад тако тешко као што је у америчким метрополама Њујорку и Чикагу?

Ретко би ко од оних што долазе из Америке на то питање боље да одговори од нашег епископа у Сједињеним Државама и Канади г. Мардарија, који је прошлог повеленоника допутовао за Америке и који нам је тако рељефно изложио садашње тешко стање наших исељеника. Јер г. Мардарије не живи у једном месту или једном крају у Америци. Пошто су колоније наших исељеника разбацане по целој територији Сједињених Држава и Канади, г. Мардарије је стално на путовању по унутрашњости Америке. Већ петнаест година у Америци, свако прелазне дажгоста у Сједињеним Државама и сад најбоље невоље, г. Мардарије је, затим, и стањем, да чини упоређења.

Хиљаде и хиљаде празних станова

„Ево у овој малој Кочиној улици у којој ја сад станујем, рекао нам је јуче г. Мардарије, зидају се сад четири нове веће зграде, а у суседној Молеровој улици пет таквих зграда. А ја сам у Америци само за последњу годину провео близу двадесет хиљада километара, и нисам нигде приметио да се гради не само каква већа зграда већ ни обична кућица у којој би се скромно сместила једна породица.

Све је стало и мртвим сном спава. Нигде никога ни живота. У појединим местима има хиљаде и хиљаде празних станова. Откуд то празни станови? Просто стога што су раније многе породице становале у луксузним апартманима и засебним кућама, а у последње две-три године оне се споразумеју по дветтри породице да у једном стану заједничком живе, деле заједнички кирију, светиљку, огрев и телефон.

Под утиском воза ових празних кола, рекао сам своме секретару да је то узасло у чиколику станицу.
— Ово говори најречитије колико је невероватно велика криза у Америци!

Решио сам одмах да видим колико ће свет путника имати воза у Чикагу, који је крајња станица нинца оне пруге. С својим сам секретаром пребројали све оне, и констатовали да је оваг возма ниизило свега 11 путника. А композицију воза сачињавало је двеста вагона и седам обичних вагона за аут нике. Скренуо сам пажњу своме секретару да је воз имао више службеног особља но путника.

Стање Јенкија није боље но исељеника

— Имамо често прилике да читамо о незапосленим радницима у Њујорку и Чикагу — питали смо назад г. Мардарија. — Како стоји са незапосленима у унутрашњости Америке?

„Ја сам већ испричао у пропшлом напису у „Политици" какво је очајно стање наших исељеника у Америци. Ништа није боље ни стање осталих исељеника, па ни стање самих Јенкија, правих, рођених Американаца.

Тако сам запазио не само у већим центрима већ и у мањим местима локални листови отлис се одгласе у којима се млади, здрави квалификовани радници нуде за провинцију фармером да им бесплатно сати дневно раде све физичке послове — да обрађују имање, да музу краве, да чисте, само за храну и кров, без плате.

А ова армија незапослених кола је нема ни један долар за живот, оглас крстари тражеши после нипиром целе Америке, не само асфалтираним главним путевима намед великих градова, већ и спорећним сеоским стазама.

Милиони постају ноћни чувар хотела

Ова неочекивана катастрофа изнад је погодила најодговорније магнате велике и силне Америке.

У Либертивилу код Чикага син српског министра Светог Саве, центар српских насеља у Америци, буде сад на основу пре две године, уз војних агина исто годину, на прном месту нашег генијалног научника г. Михаила Пупина и генералног конзула у Америци г. Радоја Јанковића. Ту сам малопређ упознао и не исцеливно, у цркву про Светог Луке која се налази на најаристократскијем северу

Епископ г. Мардарије

Пошто моја епархија обухвата цео северни амерички континент, и доста лутујам жељезницом. До пре три године морао сам за своје и свога секретара, који сам стал на путу прати, узети увек један или дваца вечером место на спавним колима. Сада се за то нема потребе, јер се у било каквом живим кад се радни воз, чак ни за краће растојање.

Два путника у спаваним колима Пансилванске жељезнице

Пре месец дана путовао сам из Питебурга у Чикаго. Није то нека побочна, провинцијска линица, већ главна артерија америчких железница, — таквана Пансилванска железница — она директно везује Њујорк—Питебург—Чикаго. Са много пута ја сам био, као и увек путовао.

На главну станицу Невиловау жељезнице у Питебургу упознао сам ту једну познату личност и наших људи.

Ушли смо у спаваћа кола ноћ-њале. Познајем ја ту целу, толико сам пута путовао овуда но ја сам последњих петнаест година можда једном па и путовао кроз Америку! Ах путника очекивало се раније на овом огромном дворани ни да воза

(А. А.)

зак и одлазак возова свим странама света, дању и ноћу. Сада је сала аданија празна, свега неколико људи било је у њој. Препашцен, упиткивао сам:

— Воз за Чикаго измакао ми је?

— Не, имате просветенство, воз је свакако на станици, — одговорио ми је уредник америчког „Србобрана" из Питебурга г. Бранко Дзјнчић.

И заиста је воз био на станици. Група ме је допратила до самих спавајних кола. У њима никога ни живота. И те ноћи из Питебурга смо за воз 800 километара смо за ми секретар. А спавала кола у Америци су много од европских.

И Самуел Инсул остаје без посла

Као српски владика, често сам поизвлен у госте свим аристократске куће. Тако сам имао прилике да познајем и народнину чувара у једном хотелу, где сам на ту толику мери био и у мало натугбили сам што су имали, и некма су мае кад су ети што у деоби. Двојица мултомилионара, који су свако године обилно помагали оно прену, једну од најболих и научвенијих у Чикагу на путу, чак и приватних тура, на њивое туторе гда је оно моро дуну дана да тражи службу. За једнога од њих је, после стотину мука, успео да нађе место ноћног чувара у једном хотелу, са платом од 80 долара месечно.

Као такав, сер Самоел Инсул је контролисао послове у суми од четири милиарде долара. То је био један од најбеже оперисаних људи у Америци икада знаш. Пред сам мој одлазак из Чикага, пре десет дана, у мистер Инсулом затворен су и последња вратаница, од канцеларја у којима се за последњих четрдесет година налазио диктатор. Поражен, бил, он је мио воза се и очекиван се налазу упоичну:

— Ево, доће време да и Самоел Инсул остане без посла, срушив ни идеала и Алгуњског Болог.

Његово доче имање од 8.000 хектара земље, свега три километра на удар далеко од нашег, српског манастира Светог Саве у Либертину, заплењено је, и ту је на њега и других имкогуснтено мистер Самоеула. Инсула ниједан шестак на лушка имање и он владач. Иста је судбина погодила и његовог брата Мартина Инсула, сер Самоел Инсул-Млаће Самоел Инсул-Млаће свака јутро у канцеларију, где оде нека никаква шеф већ најхнове."

(А. А.)

Манастир Св. Саве у Либертивилу

диктатор највећих организација трамвајске мреже целог Чикага електричних и плинска компаније у Чикагу и целом средње западу Америке.

Као такав, сер Самоел Инсул је контролисао послове у суми од четири милиарде долара...

Хиротонисање г. Мардарија

— Јуче је на свечан начин запладичен наш први епископ америчко-канадски. —

Хиротонисање г. Мардарија.

СМРТ МАРДАРИЈА,
православног епископа америчко-канадског

Чикаго, 14 децембра
Умро је Мардарије, епископ српске цркве у Северној Америци и Канади.

Нешто пре девет часова почео је јуче у Саборној Цркви обред хиротонисања г. Мардарија, нашег првог епископа америчко-канадског. Обред су вршили Патријарх г. Димитрије, епископ далматинско-истарски г. Данило и г. Серафим, епископ струмичко-тетовски.

На старословенском језику г. Мардарије је прочитао своју заклетву којом се обвезује да ће исповедајући православље, чувати црквене каноне и одлуке седам сабора.

Од почетка богослужења присутни су, поред многобројних верних, представник Двора пуковник г. Михаило Трифуновић, отправник послова америчких Сједињених Држава г. Гордон Педок и начелник Министарства Вера г. Јанић. На певници хор Првог Београдског Певачког Друштва.

После хиротонисања млади епископ облачи први пут епископске одежде и служи прву владичанску службу, пошто се дуго предано молио пред иконом Спаситеља. Из руке Патријарха г. Мардарије прима владичански жезло, емблем пастира који има да води једно велико стадо наших исељеника и подсећа их на остављени дом.

У својој краткој речи седи Патријарх упућује младога епископа како ће својим радом што корисније послужити цркви и свом народу.

Узбуђен, дрхтавим гласом епископ Мардарије одговара Патријарху са амвона. Захваљује Богу на милости и поткрепљује своју ранију заклетву.

— Испунићу завете, које сам ти дао, Боже, у храму Твом, пред народом Твојим.

Затим евоцира своје детињство, доба када је као сиромашно ђаче обилазио исту Саборну Цркву, са жељом да цео свој живот њој посвети. Захваљује Патријарху на великој доброти коју је тада показао према црногорском детету.

Затим г. Мардарије говори о свом раду, не о прошлом већ о оном који му предстоји. Потресним речима проповеда милосрђе, љубав према ближњима. Преноси се у Нови Свет, преко недогледног океана. Открива беду наших исељеника — радника — народних мученика.

— Јер био сам међу њима. Видео сам како им пламено море ливница и фабрика сажиже тело. Силазио сам к њима у руднике и каменоломе. Њихове руке су гараве, али сам се бојао да им пружим своју. Страховао сам да не помисле да сам господин.

Млади епископ наших паћеника подсећа на поворке исељеника које су се дефиловале улицама Чикага и Њујорка, кад их је глас трубе позвао да положе своје животе од Солуна до Београда.

— Са својих облакодера чудили су се Америчани овој смерној војсци. И у чуду су ме питали: „Зар има још Срба? Јер толико их је било погинуло.

Завршио је свој говор тихим гласом. Досада им је био брат, а од данас биће им отац и добри пастир.

Народ је приступио руци владике са црном младићском брадом, док их је епископ Мардарије благосиљао.

После службе Патријарх г. Димитрије приредио је свечан ручак у част америчко-канадског. На ручку је било поред чланова Архијерејског Сабора и родбине г. Мардарија, и г. Јован Марковић, помоћник министра иностраних дела.

II
Saint Sebastian of San Francisco and Jackson

Fr. Sebastian.
(Photo courtesy Alaska State Library, Michael Z. Vinokouroff Collection, P243-1-082.)

The Life of Archimandrite Sebastian of San Francisco and Jackson

Serbian Orthodox Apostle to America

by Hieromonk Damascene (Christensen)

An Apostle of Universal Significance

BORN during the presidency of Abraham Lincoln, Archimandrite Sebastian Dabović has the distinction of being the first person born in the United States of America to be ordained as an Orthodox priest,[1] and also the first native-born American to be tonsured as an Orthodox monk. His greatest distinction, however, lies in the tremendous apostolic, pastoral, and literary work that he accomplished during the forty-eight years of his priestly ministry. Known as the "Father of Serbian Orthodoxy in America,"[2] he was responsible for the founding of the first Serbian churches in the New World. This, however, was only one part of his life's work, for he tirelessly and zealously sought to spread the Orthodox Faith to all peoples, wherever he was called. He was an Orthodox apostle of universal significance.

Describing the vast scope of Fr. Sebastian's missionary activity, Bishop Irinej (Dobrijević) of Australia and New Zealand has written: "Without any outside funding or organizational support, he carried the gospel of peace from country to country.... Concentrating much of his work in the United States, he ceaselessly traveled back and forth across the American continent, using every available mode of transportation—from stagecoach to railroad to foot. His

---

[1] Alaskan-born priests were ordained before Fr. Sebastian, but this was when Alaska was still part of Russia.

[2] Mirko Dobrijević (later Irinej, Bishop of Australia and New Zealand, "The First American Serbian Apostle—Archimandrite Sebastian Dabovich," *Again,* vol. 16, no. 4 (December 1993), pp. 13–14.

wider ministry stretched from the Aleutian Peninsula of Alaska, to Russia and Japan, to small Balkan towns on the coasts of the Black and Adriatic Seas."[3]

It is said that Fr. Sebastian baptized more people than any other Serbian priest of the Western Hemisphere.[4] St. Nikolai (Velimirović) of Žiča, Serbia, who buried Fr. Sebastian at the Žiča Monastery when the latter reposed there in 1940, called

him "a viceless man" and fittingly designated him "the greatest Serbian missionary of modern times."[5]

Preparation for Apostolic Ministry

Fr. Sebastian was born in San Francisco on June 21 (new style), 1863. His parents, Ilija and Jelena Dabović, were the first recorded Serbian immigrants to the West Coast of America. In the company of his two older siblings and his father's brother Nikolai, his parents had originally come from the village of Sasovici near Herceg Novi, at the entrance of the Bay of Kotor, Montenegro. After a long voyage (including crossing the isthmus of Panama on donkeys), they arrived in San Francisco in 1853.[6] Ilija Dabović opened a store there,

---

[3] Ibid., p. 13.

[4] John R. Palandech, Commemorative *Book of the Serbian Orthodox Church in Chicago, 1905–1955.* Quoted in Mirko Dobrijević (Bishop Irinej), p. 15.

[5] Bishop Nikolai (Velimirović), "Father Sebastian Dabovich," in *Serb National Federation Commemorative Book, 1951.*

[6] Larry Cenotto, *Logan's Alley, vol. 4: Amador County Yesterdays in Picture and Prose* (Jackson, Calif.: Cenotto Publications, 2003), p. 126.

and he and his brother Nikolai established a wholesale fruit business. Fr. Sebastian was the fourth of seven children born to Ilija and Jelena, and was given the name Jovan (John). In his later years he would write to a friend: "I am the first male child born of Serbian parents in America. Before me two of my cousins (female) were born to my uncle."[7]

An Orthodox community had formed in San Francisco six years prior to Fr. Sebastian's birth, called the "Greek-Russian Slavonian Eastern Church and Benevolent Society." The community consisted of Russians, Serbs, Greeks, and Syrians who had come to California in the first years of the Gold Rush. Since this community was not yet chartered as a parish and a priest had not yet been assigned to it, the spiritual needs of the Orthodox faithful in San Francisco were served by chaplains of the Russian Imperial Navy. In 1863 one of these chaplains, Hieromonk Kyrill from the Tikhvin Monastery in Russia, baptized the infant Jovan—the future Fr. Sebastian—in a chapel on the Russian warship *Bogatyr*, which was then anchored in the San Francisco Bay.

"Eventually," Fr. Sebastian wrote many years later,

> the Russian ships weighed their anchors. And there were no more priests here. It would seem that, left without a church or a priest, this Orthodox community should have disappeared from the face of the earth, especially in the rush for gold, for wealth. Through the mercy of God, however, this did not happen. The Orthodox—Serbs, Greeks, and Russians—lived at that time in concord, and supported each other in a brotherly manner. On all major feasts, they gathered together with those who had families, and sang religious and folk songs.[8]

In 1868, a year after the United States purchased Alaska from Russia, a Russian priest was assigned to the San Francisco Orthodox

---

[7] Letter of Fr. Sebastian Dabović to Archimandrite Georgije Kodzhić. Quoted in Mirko Dobrijević (Bishop Irinej), pp. 13–14. Bishop Irinej notes: "Fr. Sebastian... was known as the 'first Serbian child,' as he was considered to be the firstborn male of Serbian ancestry in America.... (This may not be strictly true; however, the term is used as one of endearment.)"

[8] Fr. Sebastian Dabović, *"Pravoslavnaya Tserkov v Kaliforniye"* (The Orthodox Church in California), *Amerikanskii Pravoslavnii Vestnik* (American Orthodox Herald), nos. 15–16 (April 1898). Written by Fr. Sebastian in San Francisco, February 12, 1897. Translated from Russian by Robert A. Parent.

Photograph of the Dabović family in San Francisco, ca. 1900, showing Fr. Sebastian, his mother, and all six of his brothers and sisters with their families. In the center, seated in the chair, is Fr. Sebastian's mother Jelena (his father Ilija had reposed in 1887). The clergyman at left is Fr. Sebastian. The clergyman at right is Fr. Theodore Pashkovsky, whom Fr. Sebastian married to his niece Ella in 1897. (Fr. Theodore would later become Metropolitan Theophilus, chief hierarch of the American Metropolia.) Ella is in the back row, second from the right.

community. The new pastor, Fr. Nikolai Kovrigin, had been transferred from the Russian Orthodox cathedral in Sitka, Alaska, along with an assistant, Reader Vasily Shishkin. The community in San Francisco now began to hold church services in the home of a local Serb, Peter Sekulović, located on Mission Street, which was at that time considered to be outside of town. The Dabović family attended services regularly in this house chapel, known as the "Prayer House of the Orthodox Oriental Church."

Jovan Dabović was a serious, quiet, and somewhat frail child, whose piety was manifest from an early age. He later recalled the first Divine Liturgy that Fr. Nikolai celebrated at the Sekulović home, which was evidently the first Liturgy celebrated on land (not on a ship) in San Francisco. At the time he would have been four or five years old:

I remember that first service, to which I went with my mother. We had to walk a long way along unpaved streets. Furthermore we were mercilessly drenched by rain. At last we reached a small house; we crossed over a ditch (or temporarily excavated gutter) on a plank and entered the church. The "church" was set up in a divided room. At the end, opposite the entrance, the Holy Antimension lay on a covered table. A little table in a corner served as the table of oblation. I remember two icons

Bishop John (Mitropolsky) of the Aleutians and Alaska (1836–1914)

on the walls: the Savior and the Mother of God. There were approximately twenty communicants at that Liturgy.[9]

In 1872, when Jovan was nine years old, the newly consecrated Russian bishop of Alaska and the Aleutians, John (Mitropolsky), transferred his residence from Sitka, Alaska, to San Francisco. Since he was the only Orthodox bishop for the American continent, this move marked the transfer of the entire American diocesan administration to California.

Bishop John was proficient in the English language, and came from Russia to America with the intention not only of serving the needs of the Orthodox Native Americans and Russians in Alaska, but also of bringing the Orthodox Faith to the heterodox on the North American continent. This was the primary reason why he moved the diocesan residence to California. In the midst of the large American population in San Francisco, he believed, the Orthodox Church would be able to reveal her truth to the non-Orthodox Christian confessions and to American society in general with greater effect and impact.[10] It is likely that Bishop John's desire to bring Americans from other Christian confessions into the Ortho-

[9] Ibid.
[10] Constance J. Tarasar and John H. Erickson, eds., *Orthodox America 1794–1976: Development of the Orthodox Church in America* (Syosset, New York: The Orthodox Church in America, 1975), p. 29.

dox Church was passed on to Jovan Dabović even at that early period of his life, for it became Jovan's lifelong desire, also.

In coming to San Francisco, Bishop John erected a church on Pierce Street and consecrated it as the St. Alexander Nevsky Cathedral. As often as there was a service at the cathedral, young Jovan was there. Having become wholly dedicated to the Church, he deeply loved the beauty and solemnity of Orthodox worship, and desired with all his heart to serve God and his fellow man at the holy altar. As he later affirmed, it was his intention from childhood to become a priest, and he never thought of anything else.[11]

With this in mind Jovan attended the Saturday church school and the "Graeco-Russian Seminary" (also known as the Mission School) that Bishop John had transferred from Sitka to San Francisco. At the small seminary he studied alongside Aleut natives who had come from Alaska. There he became proficient in Russian and Church Slavonic, and also gained a fair knowledge of Greek. Recalling those days in San Francisco, Fr. Sebastian wrote:

> From the time of the arrival of the Right Reverend John, priests, after his example, began to proclaim the word of truth to the flock in San Francisco. A Saturday school for the children of parishioners was opened where they were taught the Catechism and the Russian language.... Michael Vladimirov was choir director and singing teacher. He also taught mathematics at the [Mission] school. Besides the clergymen that taught at the school, Vladyka himself also had seven classes a week, in Holy Scripture and the Slavonic language. A native Greek, Dimitrios Frankiades, from the University of Athens, was teacher of the Greek and English languages.
>
> At the time of the Right Reverend John as many as sixteen pupils studied at the bishop's school in San Francisco. Of that number five are now serving in various positions of the local diocese. The Right Reverend John loved his school, one might say, with a singular love.[12]

---

[11] "An Ordination Service Held at the Greek-Russian Church Yesterday Morning," *The [San Francisco] Morning Call,* Monday, August 29, 1892, p. 2. Reprinted in *Holy Trinity Cathedral Life,* vol. 1, no. 6 (February 1994).

[12] Fr. Sebastian Dabović, "The Orthodox Church in California."

As he grew to manhood, Jovan Dabović became known not only for his love for the Church but also for his selflessness and abstinence. As Bishop Irinej writes: "Those who knew him best invariably tell of his lack of ostentation and his disdain for personal wealth or possessions. A modern St. Nicholas, Jovan felt deeply the plight of the poor and helpless, identifying so readily with them that he preferred to wear only modest apparel and eat the simplest of meals—often nothing more than milk or a little cheese—rather than to eat expensive meals and dress

Sebastian Dabović as a young deacon in San Francisco
(Photo courtesy Alaska State Library, Michael Z. Vinokouroff Collection P243-1-076.)

lavishly while others did without. Frequently he simply gave his possessions away to those in need—a pattern that persisted throughout his life."[13]

After graduating from high school in 1881, Jovan served at the San Francisco cathedral as a reader and chanter of church services, and as a Sunday school teacher. In 1884 he was assigned to work in the same capacity at St. Michael's Cathedral in Sitka, Alaska. At this time, the American diocese was without a resident bishop, since Bishop John had been called back to Russia in 1876, and his successor, Bishop Nestor (Zakkis) had died unexpectly at sea in 1882. Thus, Jovan received his appointment to serve in Alaska from Metropolitan Isidore (Nikolsky) of Novgorod, St. Petersburg and Finland, who at that time was administering the American diocese from overseas.

---

[13] Mirko Dobrijević (Bishop Irinej), p. 14.

St. Michael's Cathedral in Sitka had been established in 1848 by the great enlightener of Alaska, St. Innocent. Amidst his far-reaching missionary endeavors, St. Innocent had converted the Tlingit (Kolosh) natives in the Sitka area to the Orthodox Faith. Jovan Dabović, when assisting at the Sitka cathedral, became acquainted with native families that St. Innocent had originally evangelized. He instructed the Tlingit children in the Orthodox Faith at the church school, which thanks to him changed from having classes once a week to having them every

St. Innocent, Metropolitan of Moscow, enlightener of Alaska and Siberia (1797–1879), when he was Bishop of Kamchatka, the Kuriles and the Aleutian Islands.

Iconostasis and royal doors of St. Michael's Cathedral, Sitka, Alaska.
(Photo courtesy Alaska State Library, Michael Z. Vinokouroff Collection P243-1-038.)

day. He also held discussions about the Faith with the Tlingit adults.

As a result of his contact with the Orthodox Tlingits in Sitka, the twenty-one-year-old Jovan began some missionary work in the spirit of St. Innocent, manifesting the evangelical zeal that would become the hallmark of his life. Learning from the Tlingits in Sitka that there was another Tlingit population to the northeast that had not yet converted to Orthodox Christianity, Jovan initiated their evangelization. As the catechist of the Sitka cathedral, he organized a mis-

Kolosh (Tlingit) warrior from Baranov Island (near Sitka). Painting by Mikhail T. Tikhanov, 1818.

sion of Tlingit parishioners to bring the Orthodox Faith to the non-Christian Tlingits in the area around present-day Juneau, over a hundred miles away. Several years later he recorded:

> My assistants among the Indians—the Kolosh natives Ivan Hlyantich, Pavel Katlyeyan and others—set out for what was then a very small place, now the sizable town of Juneau, and following special instructions from me, they (and other parishioners) spread the Word and Orthodoxy—and the result of that is—the present Church of St. Nicholas in Juneau.[14]

So it happened: Within six years of the Orthodox Tlingits of Sitka beginning to evangelize the Tlingits of Juneau under Jovan Dabović's guidance, the Juneau natives began coming to Sitka for baptism. Three years later, in 1893, an Orthodox church was built in Juneau by the local natives together with Serbian gold miners who

---

[14] Fr. Sebastian Dabović to the Religious Council of the Diocese of North America in New York. Written in Los Angeles, December 2, 1915. Quoted in Bishop Sava of Shumadija, *History of the Serbian Orthodox Church in America and Canada 1891–1941* (Kragujevac, Serbia: Kalenich, 1998), p. 256.

St. Michael's Cathedral in snow, Sitka, Alaska, ca. 1900.

were then living in the area.[15] Today it is the oldest continually func-
tioning church in Alaska.[16]

Jovan's health suffered from the Alaskan climate, and so, with
the blessing of the hierarchy in Russia, he returned to San Francisco
at the end of 1887, having served for over three years in Sitka. Not
many months later, in March 1888, a new bishop was assigned to the
American diocese: Bishop Vladimir (Sokolovsky-Avtonomov).

Bishop Vladimir quickly recognized what a valuable and dedicated servant of Christ he had in young Jovan. In July of 1888, after

---

[15] The church was consecrated on June 24, 1894, by the hierarch of Alaska at that time,
Bishop Nicholas (Ziorov), who had first visited Juneau two years before.
[16] "The History of St. Nicholas Church," http://www.stnicholasjuneau.org/history.
html. See also, http://dioceseofalaska.org/html/Juneaubelltower07.html.

Jovan had recovered his health, Bishop Vladimir reassigned him as teacher of the Cathedral school in San Francisco. In December of the same year, Jovan requested to be tonsured into monasticism. Thus, on December 18/30 Bishop Vladimir tonsured Jovan a monk at the St. Nicholas Church in San Francisco, giving him the name Sebastian, since that day was the feast of St. Sebastian, the Martyr or Rome.[17] A week later, on the Feast of the Nativity of Christ,[18] he ordained Fr. Sebastian to the diaconate.[19]

Bishop Vladimir had previously served as a priest and seminary inspector in Kholm on Russia's western frontier, where many Uniates (Eastern-rite Roman Catholics) had recently been reunited with the Russian Orthodox Church. He had then served the Japanese Orthodox Mission under St. Nicholas of Japan. Fluent in Japanese, he brought his Japanese cell-attendant with him to San Francisco. It is likely that this connection with the Orthodox Church in Japan planted the idea in Fr. Sebastian of visiting Japan, which he did later in life.

Bishop Vladimir had learned from St. Nicholas of Japan that, when the Orthodox Faith is brought to new territories, it must be made available in the local languages. He became the first Orthodox hierarch in the New World to preach and serve in English; and he required his priests to learn and serve in this language as well. As Fr. Sebastian recalled: "The bishop paid special attention in the temple to preaching the word of God in English, which was the language commonly understood. To this end the bishop himself, although not completely familiar with the English language, improvised talks in English, which the people readily heard."[20] Bishop Vladimir also assigned Fr. Sebastian, as a native English speaker, to be the English-language preacher at the San Francisco cathedral.

Musically talented, Bishop Vladimir formed a superb choir at the cathedral, which he instructed to sing English translations of Orthodox services set to traditional Russian melodies. His efforts

---

[17] *San Francisco Daily Evening Bulletin,* vol. 67, no. 72, December 31, 1888.

[18] December 25, 1888/January 6, 1889. At that time there was a difference of twelve days between the old-style and new-style calendars.

[19] *San Francisco Daily Evening Bulletin,* vol. 67, no. 77, January 7, 1889.

[20] Fr. Sebastian Dabović, "The Orthodox Church in California."

Bishop Vladimir (Sokolovsky-Avtonomov)
of the Aleutians and Alaska (1852–1931).
(Photo courtesy Alaska State Library, Michael Z.
Vinokouroff Collection P243-1-004.)

attracted many people to the cathedral, which by that time had
moved to Powell Street, so that it soon became filled beyond capacity.[21] In 1888 he enlarged, remodeled, and magnificently adorned
the cathedral and dedicated it to St. Nicholas. When, in 1889, this
cathedral was destroyed by fire, Bishop Vladimir had a new cathedral built in honor of St. Basil the Great. Fr. Sebastian served as deacon in the consecration of the new cathedral.

Fr. Sebastian had great admiration for Bishop Vladimir, seeing
in him a true shepherd who gave his life for the sheep (cf. John 10:11).

---

[21] Tarasar and Erickson, p. 30.

The bishop was a man of refined, gentle character who had no regard for his personal needs, living a highly ascetical life and observing a sparse monastic diet. A missionary-minded hierarch like his predecessor Bishop John, he was the first Orthodox bishop to traverse the American continent, which he did three times in search of Orthodox communities and of non-Orthodox people to bring into the Faith. Evi-

St. Basil's Cathedral on Powell St., San Francisco.

dently inspired by his previous work with former Uniates in Russia, in 1891 he traveled to Minneapolis, Minnesota in order to receive a Uniate priest, Fr. Alexis Toth, and his parish of 350 believers into the Orthodox Church. In this way he began the return of American Uniates to Orthodoxy, a movement which would bring forth an abundant harvest in the years to come.

Fr. Sebastian, in serving under Bishop Vladimir during his formative years as a deacon, was undoubtedly influenced by the bishop's evangelical spirit, just as he had been formed earlier by the missionary vision of Bishop John.

At the end of 1890, Bishop Vladimir sent Fr. Sebastian to study at the Theological Academy in St. Petersburg, which then the imperial capital of Russia. There the young hierodeacon met the former administrator of the American diocese, the aforementioned Metropolitan Isidore of Novgorod, St. Petersburg and Finland.

Metropolitan Isidore was a major figure in the Russian Orthodox Church, and a major support of the Orthodox Church in the New World. When Fr. Sebastian was studying in St. Petersburg, the metropolitan was crowning fifty years of episcopal service, having participated in the consecration of over one hundred bishops, including all the bishops of the American mission in the latter half of

*Metropolitan Isidore (Nikolsky)
of Novgorod, St. Petersburg and
Finland (1799–1892).*

the nineteenth century. As Fr. Sebastian later wrote, the metropolitan "was the most faithful friend, spiritual advisor, and material support, under God, of the young Church in North America in her many serious trials, temptations, and persecutions." Recalling his own association with the great hierarch, Fr. Sebastian wrote: "[I] had the good fortune of obtaining [my] first official appointment to service in the ranks of the clergy from the Most Reverend Isidore[22] ... and furthermore had the spiritual consolation and privilege to obtain his personal blessing, and to kiss the hand of the greatest Prelate of the day."[23]

In the harsh northern climate of St. Petersburg, Fr. Sebastian again began to suffer health problems. Thus, in 1891 he transferred to the Theological Academy in the Ukrainian city of Kiev.[24]

The Beginning of His Apostolic Labor

In the autumn of 1891, while Fr. Sebastian was still studying in Kiev, Bishop Vladimir was called back to Russia and appointed Bishop of Ostrog. Soon thereafter he was replaced in America by the newly consecrated Bishop Nicholas (Ziorov).

[22] Here Fr. Sebastian was referring to the fact that, in 1884, Metropolitan Isidore had appointed him as reader and chanter of the Divine services in St. Michael's Cathedral in Sitka, Alaska.

[23] Fr. Sebastian Dabovich, *The Lives of the Saints, and Several Lectures and Sermons* (San Francisco: The Murdock Press, 1898), p. 3. Fr. Sebastian dedicated this, his second book, to Metropolitan Isidore, who reposed in 1892. The above quotations are taken from Fr. Sebastian's dedication.

[24] Resume of Fr. Sebastian, written in 1895, Alaskan-Russian Church Archives, *Records of the Russian Orthodox Greek Catholic Church of North America—Diocese of Alaska* (Library of Congress, Manuscript Division, 1984), container B5, reel 10.

Fr. Sebastian returned to America in April 1892, and was reassigned as a deacon of the San Francisco cathedral. On the day after the Feast of the Dormition of the Mother of God in 1892,[25] Bishop Nicholas ordained him to the holy priesthood in the St. Basil Cathedral. On the following Sunday Fr. Sebastian gave his first sermon as a priest, on the theme "Love according to Christian Doctrine."[26]

Before his ordination, Fr. Sebastian had submitted a report to Bishop Nicholas in which he estimated that there were some 1,500 Orthodox Christians residing in the states of California and Oregon, and in the then-territory of Washington. He asked that he be assigned to minister to these believers; and Bishop Nicholas, recognizing his rare apostolic zeal, granted his request.[27] Thus, the newly ordained Hieromonk Sebastian was appointed as missionary priest for California and the Pacific Northwest. Losing no time in fulfilling the task given him, within a week after his ordination he left on a missionary tour of the West Coast of North America. He traveled as far north as Vancouver, British Columbia, and as far south as San Diego, eventually covering over 3,000 miles.[28]

On this missionary journey Fr. Sebastian found poor Orthodox immigrants of many ethnic backgrounds who lived far from Orthodox churches and clergy. As he wrote in a letter to Bishop Nicholas, some of these believers had come under the influence of Protestant churches, and yet they welcomed the opportunity to return to the Church of their youth. He also found many Uniates who, although they called themselves Orthodox, had acquired what he termed questionable practices resulting from their ecclesiastical ties to Roman Catholicism.[29]

While in the Northwest Fr. Sebastian performed baptisms, both of children and adults, and offered the other Mysteries and

[25] August 16/28, 1892. See note 18 above.
[26] "An Ordination Service," p. 2.
[27] Brigit Farley, "Circuit Riders to the Slavs and Greeks: Missionary Priests and the Establishment of the Russian Orthodox Church in the American West, 1890–1910," Occasional Paper 276 (Woodrow Wilson International Center for Scholars, 2000), p. 1.
[28] Ibid.
[29] Ibid., referring to the letter of Fr. Sebastian Dabović to Bishop Nicholas, November 17, 1892, Alaskan-Russian Church Archives, *Records of the Russian Orthodox Greek Catholic Church of North America—Diocese of Alaska,* container D511/13, reel 520.

Bishop Nicholas (Ziorov) of the Aleutians and Alaska (1851–1915).
(Photo courtesy Alaska State Library, Michael Z. Vinokouroff
Collection P243-1-008.)

services of the Church to the isolated Orthodox Christians. Extremely grateful to the missionary priest, these believers began to cherish hopes that Orthodox churches would be founded in their region.

In Oregon Fr. Sebastian decided that Portland was the best site for a chapel. While he regretted that there were few Orthodox in the city itself, Portland was a central location for believers in the area. For example, a population of Greek fishermen had settled along the Columbia river and in the port city of Astoria.

In Seattle Fr. Sebastian saw even more possibilities, for there he found a core group of dedicated Orthodox Christians who were eager to form a parish. Seattle, he wrote to Bishop Nicholas, "promises to be the center of a lively parish." He also found Orthodox Christians in the communities of Tacoma, Gig Harbor, and Wilkeson, Washington, and in Vancouver and Victoria, British Columbia. In Gig Harbor he baptized the American Indian wife of a pious Serbian man from Herzegovina; this couple and their large extended family later became founding members of the first Orthodox church in Seattle.[30]

Although he was of Serbian ancestry, Fr. Sebastian knew his task was to minister to Orthodox Christians of all ethnic backgrounds, and to minister and reach out to the non-Orthodox as well. Being fluent in English, Serbian, and Russian, and knowing some Greek as well, Fr. Sebastian was a bridge between the New World and the ancient Faith of traditional Orthodox lands. In the words of Bishop Irinej: "By every report Sebastian Dabović was not one to ask about jurisdictional or national affiliation before setting out on long journeys to minister to Orthodox Christians in mining communities, lumber camps, or far-distant towns or villages. He offered his pastoral services with a free hand to anyone who was in need. Just as he gave no thought to his own comforts as a youth, caring more for the needs of others than for his own concerns, Fr. Sebastian denied himself all worldly comforts of home, family, or earthly possessions, so that he could provide for the spiritual needs of the Russian, Serbian, Bulgarian, Greek, Syrian, or Arab Orthodox Christians who required his aid."[31]

While Fr. Sebastian was serving as a missionary in the Pacific Northwest, the above-mentioned Fr. Alexis Toth was traveling from his former Uniate parish in Minneapolis to Uniate communities in Wilkes-Barre and Mayfield, Pennsylvania. Soon he succeeded in bringing these communities into the Orthodox Church as well. An outstanding missionary through whose influence and example nearly thirty thousand Uniates were eventually united to the true Church of Christ, Fr. Alexis was canonized by the Orthodox Church in America in 1994 as St. Alexis of Wilkes-Barre.

---

[30] Ibid., pp. 2, 4–5, and the letter of Fr. Sebastian Dabović to Bishop Nicholas, November 17, 1892.

[31] Mirko Dobrijević (Bishop Irinej), p. 15.

St. Alexis (Toth) of Wilkes-Barre
1853–1909.

In 1893, St. Alexis wrote to Bishop Nicholas requesting an assistant priest for St. Mary's Orthodox Church in Minneapolis, so that he could return to Pennsylvania and complete his work of bringing the Wilkes-Barre community more fully into the Orthodox ethos and way of life. Granting this request, Bishop Nicholas sent Fr. Sebastian to serve at St. Mary's Church in Minneapolis.

While at St. Mary's, Fr. Sebastian continued the work of St. Alexis, striving to help former Uniates enter more deeply into the life of the Orthodox Church. He preached eloquent sermons and taught at the parish's missionary school. The choir director of the parish and the music director of the school, Paul Zaichenko, has provided for us this valuable portrait of Fr. Sebastian in the early days of his priestly ministry:

> Fr. Sebastian Dabovich succeeded Fr. A. Toth as parish priest. He was a quiet and pensive monk, always considerate, conscientious, modest. He performed his duties sincerely, and taught the Bible class of the parish school with enthusiasm. He was a tireless and unselfish worker, a humble and a just man before his Lord. He was one of the most worthy workers in the Mission.
>
> I knew him back in San Francisco. At that time he sang in the cathedral choir, of which I was a choirmaster. His aim was his betterment in religious life. As in San Francisco, so too in Minneapolis, he was the example of virtuous living; he always considered it his duty to avoid an evil step. Leading a quiet mo-

St. Mary's Church, Minneapolis, Minnesota.

nastic life, he found great happiness in reading religious books and in teaching students the Holy Bible. He loved children and was always considerate of his parishioners. Notwithstanding his short stay in Minneapolis, he was loved by his flock. He was a bright torch of love, kindness, and sincerity.[32]

While serving at the parish in Minneapolis, Fr. Sebastian made his first visit to Chicago, where he spent ten days helping Bishop Nicholas to organize an exhibit of Orthodox Christianity at the World's Columbian Exposition (also known as the Chicago World's Fair). While in Chicago, he gathered local Orthodox Serbs and celebrated the Divine Liturgy for them. Although he was only able to

[32] *Golden Jubilee Album,* St. Mary's Russian Orthodox Church (Minneapolis, 1937), p. 44. In Tarasar and Erickson, p. 96.

The missionary school at St. Mary's Church in Minneapolis, Minnesota.

meet about twenty Serbs at that time, years later he would build upon the foundation he had laid for a Serbian Orthodox church in Chicago.[33]

In recognition of Fr. Sebastian's missionary labors, in May of 1893 Bishop Nicholas awarded him with a gold cross in Minneapolis. Although this award was normally given in the Russian Church only after ten years of priestly ministry, Fr. Sebastian received it not even a full year after his ordination to the priesthood. The reason for this was explained by Bishop Nicholas in his address to Fr. Sebastian:

> With the blessing of the Most-holy Ruling Synod of All Russia and by the assent of the Most-pious Emperor, this high sign of distinction is now bestowed upon you, my beloved brother in the Lord. It is granted to you not only as a reward for your devout ministry in the lower ecclesiastical ranks, but even more so as an encouragement in the ever greater labors and heroic tasks which you will continue to face in your missionary ministry....
>
> You were not forced to pick up the cross of a monk and a missionary, but did it of your own free will, for your and others' salvation. This made you not your own but Christ's (cf. Gal.

---

[33] Fr. Sebastian Dabović to Protopresbyter Petar Stajčić, Ravanica Monastery in Srem, 1935. *Holy Resurrection Serbian Orthodox Cathedral, 1905–2005* (Chicago, 2005), p. 48.

3:29); now you should seek not your own (cf. 1 Cor. 13:5) but the things which are Jesus Christ's (cf. Phil. 2:21).[34]

After less than a year of serving in Minneapolis, Fr. Sebastian was recalled to the West Coast to resume his missionary work there. He arrived back in San Francisco in December of 1893. Shortly thereafter he went to baptize a Serbian infant in Jackson, California, a gold-mining community near the "mother lode." Seeing that many Serbian miners had settled with their families in Jackson and in neighboring towns, Fr. Sebastian immediately recognized the need to build an Orthodox church there, and he urged the local Serbs to begin planning one. The Serbs agreed and began pooling their resources. Fr. Sebastian asked for and received a contribution from the "Kennedy Mining and Milling Company," which owned the main gold mine in Jackson. Soon the Serbs purchased land for both a cemetery and a church.[35]

In February of 1894, Bishop Nicholas came to Jackson to bless the church property; in May of the same year the first burial in the cemetery occurred; and by December the church was completed. It was a small but beautiful church, situated prominently atop the tallest hill in the town, and surrounded by the cemetery.

Bishop Nicholas had bells for the church sent down from Alaska. He also donated a chandelier, together with an icon of the Mother of God which had been painted at St. Panteleimon's Monastery on Mount Athos. In time the Mother of God would perform miracles through this icon, which would come to be known as the "Jackson Icon of the Mother of God."[36]

On December 16, Bishop Nicholas, assisted by Fr. Sebastian, consecrated the new church, dedicating it to St. Sava of Serbia. Although the service of consecration was in the Slavonic language, Fr. Sebastian—always the missionary—translated portions of the service for the non-Serbian locals in attendance.[37] The new church in

---

[34] Bishop Nicholas (Ziorov), "A Message to Hieromonk Sebastian (Dabovich) as He Is Awarded a Gold Pectoral Cross from the Office of His Majesty." Translated from Russian. First published in English in *Holy Trinity Cathedral Life,* December 20, 1992.

[35] Bishop Nikolai (Velimirović), "Father Sebastian Dabovich."

[36] The icon's feast has been appointed to be celebrated on July 12/25.

[37] Leslie McLaughlin, "St. Sava Celebrates 110 Years in Amador," *Ledger Dispatch* (October 28, 2004).

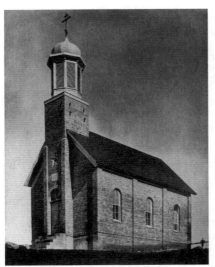

St. Sava Church, Jackson, California, as it originally looked.

Jackson, founded by the first Orthodox priest ordained in the United States, became the first Serbian Orthodox church consecrated in the Western Hemisphere. (Today the building itself has the further distinction of being the oldest standing Orthodox church in the western contiguous United States.)[38]

While remaining based in San Francisco, Fr. Sebastian regularly went to Jackson to serve at the new parish. He also continued his missionary travels throughout the western United States. In August 1894 he visited Portland and Seattle, where he had helped to organize Orthodox communities two years before. In Portland he spent a few weeks raising funds to erect a church on land donated for that purpose by Lavrenti Chernoff, an Alaskan of mixed Native-Russian ancestry. By the time Fr. Sebastian left Portland, he had succeeded in raising the needed money, and work on the new church was already in progress. In Seattle he also arranged for the erecting of a church.[39]

Fr. Sebastian's next trip northward was in February 1895. The church in Portland had by this time been completed, and Fr. Sebastian served the first Divine Liturgy there, dedicating it in the name of the "Holy and Life-giving Trinity." At that time, the small congregation consisted of six Syrians, four Serbs, and two Russians. (By 1907, the community had grown to about eighty believers.) The Orthodox church in Seattle, meanwhile, was in the process of being built, and was soon to receive its first priest, Fr. Amvrosios Vretta.[40]

[38] The original church building still serves an active parish. The parishioners are currently compiling accounts of miracles performed through the above-mentioned "Jackson Icon of the Mother of God."

[39] "A New Greek Church," *Morning Oregonian,* August 15, 1894, p. 10.

[40] Tarasar and Erickson, p. 35.

The Jackson Icon of the Most Holy Theotokos.

In his travels, Fr. Sebastian again visited the Orthodox community in Wilkeson, Washington, helping to found a parish there which later, in 1900, would build a church also dedicated to the Holy Trinity.[41] Further south, he met with groups of Serbs in Angels

[41] This church was consecrated by Bishop Tikhon (later canonized as a saint; see below) in 1902. In 1996 the parish in Wilkeson, having outgrown its church building, moved to a nearby location in Tacoma. The original church in Wilkeson remains in pristine condition,

Camp (near Jackson), California; in Fresno, California (and in the nearby towns of Visalia and Hanford); and in Bisbee, Arizona. These visits bore fruit as well, for in all of these places Serbian Orthodox churches were eventually built.[42]

Fr. Sebastian also visited isolated Orthodox Christians who had recently settled in the mining boomtown of Virginia City, Nevada.[43] When the famed Comstock silver lode was exhausted in 1898, however, the city's population declined drastically, and it is probable that the small Orthodox community moved elsewhere.

In 1896 Fr. Sebastian made a trip to his ancestral land of Serbia, where he studied theology for several months. When he returned to San Francisco in November of the same year, he was assigned as pastor of St. Basil Cathedral and as a teacher in the church school.[44] This new position did not prevent him from carrying on his missionary work throughout the western United States. He continued to visit the new communities he had formed and organized, tending to their spiritual needs, making the Holy Mysteries available to them, and ensuring their survival.

When the St. Sava Church in Jackson, California, had received full parish status, Bishop Nicholas had wanted it to be chartered as Russian Orthodox, since it was under the Russian diocese. Fr. Sebastian defended the desire of the parishioners to have their charter read "Serbian Orthodox," but also indicated that the parish would still be under the omophorion of the Russian bishop for the American mission.[45] Thus Fr. Sebastian defended the right of the Serbian community to retain its ethnic identity, and at the same time upheld the authority of the local diocesan bishop.

Interestingly, Bishop Nicholas was not against the idea of having Serbian priests and parishes in the United States subordinate to the Orthodox Church in Serbia, as long as the Serbian Church could support these priests and parishes. In 1897 both Bishop Nicholas

and is used for occasional services. After the church in Jackson, it is the oldest surviving Orthodox church building in the western contiguous United States.

[42] Farley, p. 2.
[43] Gray, p. 78.
[44] *Orthodox American Messenger,* no. 5, December 27, 1896, p. 143.
[45] Bishop Nikolai (Velimirović), "Father Sebastian Dabovich."

Metropolitan Mihailo (Jovanović)
of Serbia (1826–1898).

and Fr. Sebastian wrote to Metropolitan Mihailo (Jovanović) of Serbia, asking if this was possible. Metropolitan Mihailo replied to Fr. Sebastian:

His Grace Bishop Nicholas has written to Us and asked if We could allocate money for churches, schools, priests and teachers; and if We could, he would have nothing against there being separate Serbian priests subordinate to the Serbian Metropolitanate. And I answered that We could not do this because We could not support so many churches and priests, schools and teachers there.

I think that You should agree to this and listen to Your Bishop, and he will help You and protect the Serbs and Orthodoxy, and will not destroy Serbian national customs.[46]

In reply, Fr. Sebastian wrote to Metropolitan Mihailo:

I have received Your well-intentioned letter and I completely understand. I bow before You and thank You sincerely. I shall be guided by Your advice. Orthodoxy progresses in America. Serbs are found in various states, they are being revived spiritually and communicate with our organization.[47]

In August of 1897, Fr. Sebastian traveled to Butte, Montana. At that time the center of the nation's copper-mining industry, the western boomtown of Butte was the home of a large number of Serbs who had come to work in the mines. On the Feast of the Dormition Fr. Sebastian celebrated the first Divine Liturgy in the history of Butte, and afterwards he met with the thirty-one Serbs in

[46] Serbian Metropolitan Mihailo to Hieromonk Sebastian. Written in Belgrade, October 24, 1897. Quoted in Bishop Sava, p. 23.

[47] Hieromonk Sebastian to Metropolitan Mihailo of Serbia. Written in San Francisco, December 14, 1897. Quoted in Bishop Sava, pp. 23–24.

attendance in order to organize a parish there. He followed up on this visit by traveling to Butte four to six times a year to serve the Divine Liturgy and observe the progress of the parish.[48]

At the end of October in 1897, Fr. Sebastian and Fr. Alexander Hotovitsky—a Russian priest from New York, later canonized as a New Martyr of Russia—accompanied Bishop Nicholas on a trip to Washington, D.C. Fathers Sebastian and Alexander served as translators when Bishop Nicholas met with President William McKinley. This was the second meeting in the history of the United States between an Orthodox bishop and a U.S. president (the first having been a meeting between Bishop Vladimir and President Grover Cleveland in 1889).[49] In his audience with President McKinley, Bishop Nicholas expressed his concern over the treatment of Orthodox Christians in Alaska, particularly over the fact that American trading companies were compelling the faithful to work on Sundays and feast days and had unlawfully taken possession of Church properties. The president promised to bring the matter before Congress.[50]

On November 9, 1897, soon after returning to his post at the San Francisco cathedral, Fr. Sebastian officiated at the wedding of his niece, Ella, to a young Russian immigrant, Theodore Pashkovsky.[51] His new son-in-law was ordained to the priesthood less than a month afterward. Many years later, following the repose of Ella, Fr. Theodore Pashkovksy would be tonsured a monk with the name Theophilus, consecrated a bishop, and eventually (in 1934) elected as the Metropolitan of All America and Canada for the American Metropolia.[52]

---

[48] Reader Alexander Vallens, "Archimandrite Sebastian Dabovich: The First American Serbian Orthodox Apostle" (2005), p. 5. http://www.transfigcathedral.org/ faith/corner/ Dabovich.pdf.

[49] *Tserkovniye Vedomosti* (Church Gazette), 1889, no. 10, p. 262. During his meeting with President Cleveland, Bishop Vladimir reported on the condition of his flock in Alaska. See Bishop Gregory (Afonsky), *A History of the Orthodox Church in Alaska 1794–1917* (Kodiak, Alaska: St. Herman's Theological Seminary Press, 1977), pp. 82–83.

[50] "Bishop Nicholas' Complaint," *Washington Post,* November 5, 1897. In Tarasar and Erickson, p. 73.

[51] "An Orthodox Ceremony," *The San Francisco Call,* Tuesday, November 9, 1897.

[52] Tarasar and Erickson, p. 200.

Serving under St. Tikhon

The year 1898 brought a great blessing for Orthodoxy in America, when Bishop Tikhon (Bellavin) was appointed by the Russian Orthodox Church to head the American diocese. A farsighted apostle of Christ, Bishop Tikhon would later become the Patriarch of Moscow and all Russia, and would eventually be canonized by the Russian Orthodox Church.

On December 23, 1898, St. Tikhon arrived at his new cathedral city of San Francisco. He was met at the train station by Fr. Sebastian, by Hieromonk John Shamie (a Syrian priest from the Orthodox mission in Galveston, Texas), and by representatives of the various nationalities of the cathedral parish: Russian, Serbian, Greek, and Syro-Arab.[53] Bishop Tikhon was at that time the only Orthodox bishop of the North American continent, the head of a vast multilingual and multiethnic missionary diocese.

By the time Bishop Tikhon came to America, Fr. Sebastian had become well known as a missionary not only at home but also abroad. In 1899 Fr. Sebastian received the Order of St. Anne from the Tsar of Russia, Nicholas II. This order had been conferred on him through the influence of Bishop Nicholas, who, on returning to Russia the previous year, had had an audience with the Tsar and had recommended Fr. Sebastian for the award.[54]

Two years earlier, in 1897, Fr. Sebastian had been awarded the Order of Daniel from Prince Nicholas of Montenegro, primarily in recognition of the pastoral care he had shown for Serbian immigrants who had come to America from Montenegro, and also for the articles he had written on the province of Montenegro and its struggles against the Turks.[55] According to the testimony of St. Nikolai of Žiča, Fr. Sebastian was also given awards by the King of Serbia and the Patriarch of Jerusalem.[56]

Toward the end of the nineteenth century, Fr. Sebastian somehow found time, amidst his already abundant labors, to develop one

---

[53] Ibid., p. 85.
[54] "Rev. Sebastian Dabovich Honored by the Czar of Russia," *The San Francisco Call*, Wednesday, June 17, 1899.
[55] Ibid.
[56] Bishop Nikolai (Velimirović), "Father Sebastian Dabovich."

St. Tikhon (1865–1925) when he was Bishop of the Aleutians and Alaska.

of the first English translations of the Orthodox Divine Liturgy,[57] and also to write three English-language books on the Orthodox Faith: *The Holy Orthodox Church: The Rituals, Services, and Sacraments of the Eastern Apostolic (Greek-Russian) Church* (1898); *Lives of the Saints, and Several Lectures and Sermons* (1898); and *Preaching in the Russian Church: Lectures and Sermons by a Priest of the*

Holy Orthodox Church (1899). In addition, he wrote articles on Orthodoxy in Alaska and California, and on Orthodox traditions surrounding the Feast of the Nativity of Christ.

In 1897, as he was completing his first book, *The Holy Orthodox Church,* Fr. Sebastian wrote about it to the above-mentioned Metropolitan Mihailo of Serbia:

> In a few days I shall finish a book, which I am writing in English—17 chapters and a foreword—about the Orthodox Church, its rites, symbolism, liturgy, and sacraments, and how it differs from the Roman and Protestant churches, etc. If His Grace Nicholas blesses the publication of this book, I think and hope to God that it will be of use to the East and West, since I am fairly well acquainted with both.[58]

(When Metropolitan Mihailo reposed in 1898, shortly before this book was published, Fr. Sebastian included in the book these words of dedication: "To the sacred memory of the late Metropolitan Michael of Serbia, by his dutiful son in the spirit, the author.")

Published with money from his own small salary, Fr. Sebastian's books bore witness to the missionary vision of their author. As his letter to Metropolitan Mihailo makes clear, they were intended to serve as books of basic Orthodox instruction, written for second- and third-generation immigrants from Orthodox lands, most of whom had English as their first language, and also for non-Orthodox who were interested in the Orthodox Church. While such books are common today, at the end of the nineteenth century they were a rarity and far ahead of their time. Anglicans, Episcopalians and others had by then translated and published some English-language books on Orthodoxy, but the Orthodox themselves had published very few expositions of the Orthodox Faith in English. Fr. Sebastian understood that, for the growth of Orthodoxy in America, this situation had to change—that the Orthodox Faith had to be taught and preached, not only in the languages of traditional Orthodox countries but also in the common language of the new country.

---

[58] Hieromonk Sebastian to Metropolitan Mihailo of Serbia. Written in San Francisco, December 14, 1897. Quoted in Bishop Sava, pp. 23–24.

Photographs of Fr. Sebastian printed in *The San Francisco Call.*

Top left: printed June 16, 1899.
Top right: October 20, 1905.
Bottom left: April 22, 1900.

Fr. Sebastian's books bear witness as well to his ardent love for Jesus Christ and His Church, to the depth of his knowledge of the Orthodox Faith, to his careful adherence to the teachings of the Church, to his pastoral zeal, to his literary and poetic gifts, and to his profound sense of spiritual beauty. A large portion of the books consists of sermons that he gave in the San Francisco cathedral and in mission churches on various feast days. These sermons reveal him as an inspired preacher whose words could soar to the heights and at the same time strike deeply the hearts of his listeners. Consider, for example, these words from a sermon he delivered on Holy Friday:

> He Who prayed, *Father, forgive them, for they know not what they do,* has stretched out His arms on the wood in order to embrace a sinful world. But no mortal knoweth how *the Word was with God, and the Word was God.* The Word of God is not bound by death. As a word from the lips dies not entirely away at the moment its sound ceases, but rather gathers new strength, and passing through the senses penetrates the minds and hearts of the hearers, so also the Hypostatical Word of God, the Son of God, in His saving incarnation, whilst dying in the flesh, fills all things with His spirit and might. Thus when Christ waxeth faint and becometh silent on the Cross, then is it that heaven and earth raise their voice to Him, and the dead preach the resurrection of the Crucified, and the very stones cry out.[59]

In other sermons included in his books, Fr. Sebastian shows himself to be a sensitive observer of the spirit of the times. His sermon "The Condition of Society" is seen to be especially prophetic today, over a century after he wrote it.[60] In it, he lamented the rise of new trends in society that indicated an apostasy from the traditional Christian way of life: the "craze after unwholesome fashions"; the "nervous, unsteady rush to 'keep up with the times,'" in which parents are in such a hurry, and are so empty inside, that they deprive their children of a stable, secure Christian home; the exaltation of shamelessness among young women, and the disdain of the virtues

[59] Fr. Sebastian Dabovich, *Preaching in the Russian Church* (San Francisco: Cubery and Company, 1899), p. 130.
[60] See Part III below.

of modesty and purity; the disrespect of young men toward their elders; the rising number of young people who wish to remain unmarried, and of married people who do not want to have children so that they can have as much pleasure as possible. "In view of all this," Fr. Sebastian said in his sermon, "the preacher of the Word of God is obliged by a terrible oath he has given before he received the gift of Apostolic succession at his ordination, to present to you the whole of the Truth, not a part of it."[61]

As an Orthodox preacher of the Gospel to the modern world, Fr. Sebastian boldly challenged the unbelief that was increasing in his day and that has only continued to grow during the following century. His books included a lengthy treatise entitled "The Authenticity and Truthfulness of the Gospel," in which he defended the historicity of the Gospel narratives; an article called "The Necessity for Divine Revelation, and the Indications of a Revealed Religion," in which he showed why the Christian Faith alone is the full and unadulterated revelation of God; and an essay on "The Immortality of the Soul," in which he demonstrated that, contrary to the view of modern materialists, the soul indeed lives on and is active after the body dies, even as the body awaits the General Resurrection.[62]

Fr. Sebastian's books also reveal how much he valued and venerated his holy missionary predecessors in America, Saints Herman and Innocent of Alaska. In one place, he included the name "Ghermanus of Alaska" in a list of particularly illustrious saints.[63] This is striking in a book published in 1898—seventy-two years before the humble monk Herman was formally glorified as a saint by the Orthodox Church. In yet another book, Fr. Sebastian included an address he had delivered at the San Francisco cathedral on August 26, 1897, on the occasion of the centennial of the birth of St. Innocent of Alaska. St. Innocent, who had reposed in Russia eighteen years before, was still remembered by some of the Orthodox Christians then in San Francisco. At the request of Bishop Nicholas, Fr. Sebas-

---

[61] Fr. Sebastian Dabovich, *Preaching in the Russian Church,* pp. 160–62.

[62] Ibid., pp. 9–63.

[63] Fr. Sebastian Dabovich, *The Holy Orthodox Church: The Rituals, Services, and Sacraments of the Eastern Apostolic (Greek-Russian) Church* (Wilkes-Barre, Pennsylvania, 1898), p. 74.

tian had produced the first English translation of the Life of St. Innocent, which was presented at the centennial celebrations.[64] In his address, Fr. Sebastian proclaimed: "*Innocentius:* My whole being thrills with a veneration at the sound of that name.... I become bold and venture to look into the unseen, where I behold the spiritual eyes of our first hard-working Missionary, with kindly light beaming upon this gathering."[65] Again, these words are all the more remarkable considering that they were uttered a full eighty years before St. Innocent's canonization. Undoubtedly, Fr. Sebastian looked on both uncanonized saints, Herman and Innocent, as models of emulation and as heavenly helpers in his own apostolic labors in America.

It was not merely through his books that Fr. Sebastian sought to introduce non-Orthodox Americans to the Orthodox Faith. According to Bishop Irinej, Fr. Sebastian "spoke tirelessly to countless individuals, making friends on all levels of society—from the common man on the street to the highest strata of American social, political, and religious life."[66]

Ever seeking to reach out to those outside the Church, Fr. Sebastian initiated contacts and discussions with non-Orthodox churches. He made his greatest efforts in the direction of the Episcopalian Church, which, at the turn of the twentieth century, he saw as the most similar to the Orthodox Church among non-Orthodox American confessions, and also as the church most receptive to Orthodoxy. As early as 1865, two years after Fr. Sebastian's birth, the ober-procurator of the Holy Synod of the Russian Church had noted that an Orthodox church was needed in San Francisco not only to provide for the residents who were already Orthodox but also "to answer to the growing interest in the Orthodox Faith among American Episcopalians."[67] Having grown up in San Francisco and having been entrusted with the apostolic ministry of the holy priesthood, Fr. Sebastian now sought to address this need. He met several times

[64] *American Orthodox Messenger,* no. 2, September 15–27, 1897, pp. 45–46. In Russian.

[65] Fr. Sebastian Dabovich, *The Lives of the Saints, and Several Lectures and Sermons* (San Francisco: The Murdock Press, 1898), pp. 164–66.

[66] Mirko Dobrijević (Bishop Irinej), p. 15.

[67] Tarasar and Erickson, p. 33.

with Bishop Charles Grafton, Episcopalian bishop of Fond du Lac, Wisconsin, and was instrumental in organizing a conference of Orthodox-Episcopalian dialogue in Fond du Lac.[68] In November of 1900, Bishop Tikhon, together with Fr. Sebastian and Fr. John Kochurov, rector of the Chicago cathedral and future New Martyr of Russia, attended the consecration of a vicar for Bishop Grafton.[69] Three years later Bishop Grafton made a trip to Russia to experience the Orthodox Church there firsthand.[70]

In all of his meetings with Episcopalians, Fr. Sebastian was sympathetic, respectful and understanding, appreciating the points in which Episcopalian doctrine and practice still reflected the original Orthodox Faith. At the same time, however, he was firmly convinced that he must reveal the Orthodox Church as the one, true Church of Christ.

This loving yet firm approach to the non-Orthodox confessions can be found in his books. At the beginning of his book, *Preaching in the Russian Church,* he placed as the epigraph the words of the Apostle Paul, *Speaking the truth in love* (Eph. 4:15)—a saying that he clearly took as his guiding principle in reaching out to those not in the Church.[71] In the same book, having presented the above-mentioned articles establishing that the soul is immortal, that Christianity is the true Faith, and that the Gospels are historically verifiable, he followed with an essay entitled "The True Church of Christ," in which he painstakingly laid out the reasons why the Orthodox Church, and no other, is the true Church.[72] Elsewhere, in an essay entitled "Sincere Religion," he said it was "foul treachery" for Orthodox Christians to make no distinction between the teachings of the different churches, and to deny that the Orthodox Church alone teaches Christ's truth purely and completely. "You will say," he

---

[68] Mirko Dobrijević (Bishop Irinej), p. 15.

[69] Vallens, p. 6.

[70] Fr. Sebastian Dabovich, "The Madonna of Alaska: A Tale of the Greek-Russian Church in Many Lands" [an overview of Orthodox Nativity traditions], *The San Francisco Sunday Call,* Christmas Number, December 20, 1903, sec. 2, p. 1.

[71] Fr. Sebastian Dabovich, *Preaching in the Russian Church,* p. 4.

[72] Ibid., pp. 64–77; see Part III below. This article was reprinted in *The Orthodox Word,* no. 5 (1965), pp. 182–87, along with an article by Eugene (later Fr. Seraphim) Rose: "Archimandrite Sebastian Dabovich and the Orthodox Mission to America" (ibid., p. 181).

wrote, "shall we then condemn our erring brethren? By no means. Christ forbids us to judge anybody, for only God knows whether our brother culpably holds the error, or whether he believes it to be the truth. But even if he believes his error to be the truth, error remains error, and can never become truth. Therefore, we must always condemn error, though we may not condemn the person erring."[73]

Although Fr. Sebastian's efforts to bring Episcopalians into the Orthodox Church did not prove successful during his lifetime, St. Tikhon later noted that Fr. Sebastian was greatly responsible for making non-Orthodox Christians, particularly Episcopalians, aware of the teachings of the Orthodox Church.[74] According to one biographer of Fr. Sebastian, some of the Western Rite parishes that were received many years later into the Antiochian Orthodox Archdiocese of North America pointed to these early efforts of Fr. Sebastian as a significant stepping-stone in the return of Episcopalians to the Orthodox Church.[75]

From the beginning of his time in America, St. Tikhon had recognized Fr. Sebastian's abilities as a missionary pastor. In 1900 he appointed Fr. Sebastian to the North American Ecclesiastical Consistory, which was the diocesan council of the entire American mission.[76] Then, in 1902, he appointed him as the Dean of the Sitka Deanery and the superintendent of Alaskan missions. Thus, after an absence of eighteen years, Fr. Sebastian returned to Alaska. He served the Sitka Deanery for two years, during which time St. Tikhon elevated him to the rank of abbot.

During his time in Alaska Fr. Sebastian made contact with a group of Serbian and Russian miners in Douglas, near Juneau, and quickly set about providing an Orthodox church for them. Land was donated by the local mining company, and a donation for the church's construction was sent from the Holy Assembly of Bishops in Serbia. Fr. Sebastian built the church with his own hands, working together with the local Orthodox Christians. On July 23, 1903,

---

[73] Fr. Sebastian Dabovich, *The Lives of the Saints, and Several Lectures and Sermons*, p. 181.

[74] St. Tikhon's communication to the Holy Synod of the Russian Orthodox Church of June 2, 1902, no. 74 (summarized below).

[75] Vallens, pp. 7–8.

[76] Gray, p. 78.

St. Sava Church, Douglas, Alaska.
(Photo courtesy Alaska State Library, Michael Z. Vinokouroff Collection P243-2-026a.)

Fr. Sebastian, along with Hieromonk Anthony (Deshkevich-Koribut) and the priest Aleksandar Jarošević, consecrated the Church of St. Sava in Douglas.[77]

Upon leaving Alaska in 1903, Fr. Sebastian went to Chicago, Illinois, where he continued the work he had initiated a decade earlier of establishing a Serbian parish. On this trip he met many more Serbs than he had during his first trip to the city. He stayed for a week and served the Divine Liturgy for them. A number of families pledged their support in building a church.

During the same year Fr. Sebastian also paid another visit to the Serbian community in Butte, Montana, encouraging the parishioners to raise money to build a church and obtain a resident priest. Then, after a brief stay in San Francisco, he left on a trip to Russia and Serbia.

Within four months after Fr. Sebastian's visit, the parishioners in Butte, Montana were able to raise enough money to start building a temple dedicated to the Holy Trinity. The church was com-

---

[77] Fr. Sebastian Dabović to the Religious Council of the Diocese of North America in New York. Written in Los Angeles, December 2, 1915. Quoted in Bishop Sava, p. 256 (see also pp. 43, 240). In 1937 the church in Douglas burned down, but the Serbian cemetery still remains nearby.

Interior of St. Sava Church, Douglas, Alaska.
(Photo courtesy Alaska State Library, Michael Z. Vinokouroff Collection P243-2-026b.)

pleted in the fall of 1904, and on the Feast of the Beheading of St. John the Forerunner, August 29/September 11, Fr. Sebastian served the first Divine Liturgy in the new church, assisted by the Serbian priest, Hieromonk Jacob (Odžić). On Vidovdan, June 15/28, 1905, St. Tikhon consecrated the Holy Trinity Serbian Orthodox Church in Butte, assisted by Fr. Sebastian and by Fr. Jacob, who became the church's first permanent priest.[78]

Due to the growth and diversity of the American diocese, St. Tikhon had by this time begun to restructure it with the blessing of the Holy Synod in Russia. In 1903 he transferred the diocesan see from San Francisco to New York and assisted in the consecration of a Russian vicar bishop for Alaska, Bishop Innocent (Pustynsky). At the same time, in the Orthodox spirit of *sobornost* (catholicity), he sought to provide for the needs of his multiethnic Orthodox flock in America, realizing that each ethnic group required special attention and leadership. As he wrote to the Holy Synod in Russia in 1905: "We do not consider that we have the right to interfere with the national character of the churches in this country; on the con-

---

[78] Vallens, p. 5. This church building served the congregation for sixty years, until the opening of a new copper mine forced the razing of the entire area. A new church, also dedicated to the Holy Trinity, was built at another location, and was consecrated by Bishop Grigorije (Udicki) in July 1965. (See Bishop Sava, pp. 257–58.)

The original Holy Trinity Church in Butte, Montana.

trary, we try to preserve it, giving each a chance to be governed by leaders of the same nationality."[79] With this in mind, in 1904 he took part in consecrating Archimandrite Raphael (Hawaweeny), later canonized as St. Raphael of Brooklyn, as a vicar bishop for the Syro-Arab Orthodox churches in America.

[79] Quoted in *Holy Resurrection Serbian Orthodox Cathedral, 1905–2005,* p. 52.

Fr. Sebastian with other missionaries, ca 1902. Left to right: Fr. Dmitri Kamnev; Abbot Innokenty (Pustynsky), future auxiliary bishop of St. Tikhon in America; St. Alexis (Toth); Deacon Vladimir Alexandrov; Abbot Sebastian Dabović. Standing: General Skliarevich, a Russian engineer.

Fr. Sebastian with fellow Serbs in America, ca. 1905. Left to right: Hieromonk Jacob (Odžić), the first permanent priest at Holy Trinity Church, Butte, Montana; Hierodeacon Damjan (Grujić); Archimandrite Sebastian (Dabović); poet Proka Jovkić, who wrote enthusiastically in the San Francisco-based newspaper *Srpska Nezavisnost* about Fr. Sebastian's work in Chicago; Priest Paja Radosavljević.

The original Holy Resurrection Church on Fowler Street in Chicago.

St. Tikhon also planned to consecrate a vicar bishop for the Serbian Orthodox churches in America. In March 1905 he established the Serbian Orthodox Mission in America, centered in Chicago. Anticipating that Fr. Sebastian, like St. Raphael for the Arabs, would become the bishop for this mission, he transferred him to Chicago and placed him in charge of the Serbian Orthodox Mission. At the same time he appointed him as the parish priest of the Serbs in Chicago, although they did not yet have a church.

A year earlier, in 1904, Fr. Sebastian had made a third visit to Chicago, spending two weeks with the Serbs there and again celebrating the Divine Liturgy for them. Now, as the acting Serbian Orthodox priest for the city, he came there for the fourth time to stay. He lost no time in fulfilling his long-held goal of founding a church for the Serbian community. Soon after his arrival in June of 1905, he served the Divine Liturgy in a rented hall on Milwaukee Avenue, with about two hundred Serbian families in attendance. Immediately afterward, he organized a parish committee and began looking for a building suitable for the new church. Within a matter of days, the first Serbian Orthodox church in the city had been established. As he later recalled:

> After some days we found a place for the new church, which was located at 8 Fowler Street,[80] on the corner of Evergreen and across from Wicker Park. We put down a $1,000 deposit (donated by Acim Lugonja). The remaining $6,500 was to be paid with interest. We created an improvised chapel immediately, made an iconostasis, and raised a cross on the building, all with-

[80] In 1936–1937, the address was changed to 1950 West Schiller Street.

in several days. The first Liturgy was held, and the church was consecrated to the Resurrection of our Lord Jesus Christ, on the 4th of July, 1905.[81]

On September 18, 1905, St. Tikhon raised Fr. Sebastian to the rank of archimandrite at the Holy Resurrection Serbian Orthodox Church in Chicago. In the words he addressed to Fr. Sebastian on this occasion, two things are evident: first of all, the genuine love and concern that this wise hierarch had for the Serbian flock in America, and secondly the great esteem he had for Fr. Sebastian in entrusting to him the spiritual guidance of the entire Serbian Mission. To Fr. Sebastian he said:

> I greet you, most honorable Father Archimandrite Sebastian, with your elevation to the rank of archimandrite and your as-signment as head of the Serbian Mission in America. You were entrusted by the diocesan authorities even earlier, as a native Serb, with the administration of one or another of the Serbian parishes here. Now you are being called to a greater ministry: upon you is being laid the care of all the Serbian churches in our extensive diocese and of the spiritual needs of all the Serbs in America. You know how many of them are scattered here, how often they go astray like sheep that have no shepherd, how they end up in a foreign home, and how, having come here for work or to become rich, some of them become spiritually impover-ished and, in this heterodox country, lose the great spiritual trea-sure of the old country: the holy Orthodox Faith, love for the Slavic people, and fondness for their good native customs. Our benevolently solicitous hierarchy, which is always concerned about the needs of the Slavs, who are of one blood with us, de-sires to have mercy on these people, and is calling upon you now to spiritually guide the Serbs who are living here.[82]

---

[81] Fr. Sebastian Dabović to Protopresbyter Petar Stajčić, Ravanica Monastery in Srem, 1935. The church building on Fowler Street served the parish until 1932, when a new church was built on the same spot. A *Chicago Tribune* article from 1932 stated that only two build-ings were being built in the city at that time, in the midst of the Great Depression: one was the post office, and the other was Holy Resurrection Church. In 1964 the church was el-evated to the title of Cathedral, and in 1975 a new church building was consecrated for the congregation on Redwood Drive.

[82] *Slovo Pravoslaviya v Amerike: Propovedi i poucheniya Svyatitelya Tikhona* (The Word of Orthodoxy in America: Sermons and Teachings of Holy Hierarch Tikhon) (Moscow: Sretensky Monastery, 2001), pp. 143–44. Translated from Russian.

A 1906 issue of the *Herald of the Serbian
Church in North America.*

The newly elevated Archimandrite Sebastian served as rector
of the church he had founded in Chicago. During his time as head
of the Serbian Orthodox Mission, he tended to the needs of the
many Serbian communities throughout the country. He also initiated the publication of the *Herald of the Serbian Church in North
America,* the first Serbian Church newspaper in the United States.

In 1905 St. Tikhon entrusted Fr. Sebastian with the task of procuring written permission from the hierarchy in Serbia for the consecration of a vicar bishop for the Serbian Orthodox Mission. Taking this task very seriously, Fr. Sebastian wrote letters to Patriarch
Georgije and to the Holy Synod of Bishops in Serbia, asking for a
letter confirming that, as far as they were concerned, there was no
obstacle to the appointment of a bishop for the Serbs in North
America. The hierarchy in Serbia, however, not knowing firsthand
the situation of Serbs in America, and also not being certain of the

relationship between the Russian and Serbian hierarchies in the context of America, replied that they were not prepared to send such a letter to the Holy Synod of Bishops in Russia. Meanwhile, some Serbian congregations in America, not wanting to be under the Russian Church even if they could have a Serbian vicar bishop, were appealing directly to bishops in Serbia for archpastoral support and direction.[83]

The Holy Synod of the Russian Church honored St. Tikhon with the title of archbishop in 1905, and two years later assigned him as to the see of Yaroslavl. Thus, St. Tikhon left America with many of his plans for the American archdiocese unrealized. Before his departure for Russia, he did not neglect to show his appreciation for Fr. Sebastian's many labors. As St. Nikolai of Žiča records:

> Archimandrite Dabovich could have been a bishop even in 1907. The Russian archbishop wanted to consecrate him as a Russian bishop for the Serbian people. But the Serbs did not want it that way. Archbishop Tikhon was sorry about that. He was eager to show his appreciation to Fr. Dabovich for all his wonderful work. Failing to make him a bishop, he did something else. Once when he celebrated the Holy Liturgy in the Serbian church in Chicago, he presented our archimandrite with a precious mitre, which was worth 1,000 roubles in gold. But Fr. Dabovich quickly sold that precious gift and gave it to the church towards paying its debts. Such a man was he. He was absolutely unselfish.[84]

"The Beginning of Sorrows" (Matt. 24:8)

In 1908 Archbishop Platon (Rozhdestvensky) replaced St. Tikhon as the archbishop of the American archdiocese. Fr. Sebastian hoped that the new archbishop would offer the same support to the Serbian Orthodox Mission as had his predecessor. In September of 1908, he wrote to Archbishop Platon, outlining the needs of the Serbian congregations in America:

---

[83] Bishop Sava, pp. 29–30.
[84] Bishop Nikolai (Velimirović), "Father Sebastian Dabovich."

Last Easter in three churches there were no services, a fourth was closed, and many colonies with a fairly dense Orthodox population did not even hear 'Christ is Risen.' It is impossible to obtain priests anywhere, and in most cases people cannot give enough to support a priest properly. Now they have promised me in Belgrade that at the next Assembly of Bishops they will raise the question of allocating two scholarships for the Mission, so that two Serbian lads from America may be educated at a seminary in Serbia. But this presents other problems: finding the money to send these lads to Europe.

Archbishop Platon (Rozhdestvensky)
(1866–1934).

Serbian archpastors in the Old Country with brotherly love expect Your Eminence to organize our part of the Church. The Lord's blessing will doubtless be given to a continuation of the work begun with wisdom, after six years of responsibility, by His Eminence Tikhon, now Archpastor of Yaroslavl.[85]

During the same year, Fr. Sebastian, while retaining his position as head of the Serbian Orthodox Mission, served at the Holy Transfiguration Church in Denver, Colorado, a parish that had been received into the Orthodox Church from Uniatism in 1904. The parish consisted primarily of Russians and Serbs. In September of 1908, Fr. Sebastian wrote to Archbishop Platon: "Here the church is fairly large, there is enough land, the debt is small.... Many children. They want a psalm-reader and teacher, who can direct a choir.... Come, Your Eminence, to Denver."[86]

[85] Archives of the American Orthodox Church, no. 1129, July 23, 1908. Quoted in Bishop Sava, p. 216.

[86] Fr. Sebastian Dabović to Archbishop Platon. Written in Denver, Colorado, September 29, 1908. Quoted in Bishop Sava, p. 278.

Since the Cathedral of St. Basil in Fr. Sebastian's native city of San Francisco had been destroyed in the great earthquake of 1906, a new cathedral, dedicated to the Holy Trinity and located at Green and Van Ness, had been built. In July of 1909 Archimandrite Sebastian traveled to San Francisco in order to consecrate the new cathedral.

In the meantime, Fr. Sebastian was experiencing a growing sense of futility as the head of the Serbian Orthodox Mission. Many Serbs in America had made it clear to him that they did not wish to support or be united under the Serbian Orthodox Mission because it was within the jurisdiction of the Russian Church. Some Serbs were even unfavorable toward Fr. Sebastian because he was under the Russian Church and had placed Serbian congregations in America under that Church.[87] Calling the Serbian Orthodox Mission "a totally Russophile agency,"[88] they accused Fr. Sebastian himself of being a "Russophile."[89]

In reality, Fr. Sebastian, as a selfless servant of Christ in His Church, cared first of all for the spiritual well-being and salvation of Christ's flock. He followed the words of His Master: *Feed my sheep* (John 21:16–17). Like St. Tikhon, Fr. Sebastian knew that, for the Serbian flock in America to be fed properly, they needed a Serbian archpastor and Serbian priests who spoke their language and understood their needs. This was the reason behind his attempt, at St. Tikhon's behest, to organize the Serbian Orthodox Mission and to have a Serbian bishop consecrated for America. Fr. Sebastian was also completely open to the possibility of Serbian congregations in America being placed under the Serbian Church; however, as we have seen, at that time the Serbian Church was not yet ready to take full responsibility for priests and parishes in America. As far as Fr. Sebastian was concerned, the most pressing question was not what Local Orthodox Church—Russian or Serbian—the Serbs in America would be under (as long as they were under a canonical hierarchy), but rather how their spiritual needs would be met, how they would be nourished by the life and grace of the Church.

---

[87] Bishop Sava, pp. 34, 40.

[88] Serbian Church-School Congregation in Steelton, Pennsylvania, to Serbian Patriarch Georgije, October 19, 1905. Quoted in Bishop Sava, p. 30.

[89] *Holy Resurrection Serbian Orthodox Cathedral,* 1905–2005, p. 51.

Holy Trinity Cathedral
in San Francisco.

Fr. Sebastian was greatly saddened that, at the end of the first decade of the twentieth century, the needs of the Serbs were *not* being met properly. For the nineteen chartered Serbian parishes in America (not to mention the smaller Serbian Orthodox communities), there were only eleven canonical priests. Non-canonical priests from Serbia took advantage of this situation, roaming the United States and performing services in Serbian communities without the blessing of any bishop. With no Serbian bishop assigned to America, and with many Serbs not wanting to be in the jurisdiction of the Russian Church, there was little Fr. Sebastian could do to stop this non-canonical activity.[90] He was placed in the unenviable position of having to defend the canonical authority of the Russian hierarchy over American Serbs (because that was indeed the canonical authority at the time) despite the fact that many Serbs resented this authority, and despite the fact that he himself knew that the Serbian churches in America were at an impasse without their own bishop.

Seeing that some Serbian priests and congregations were avoiding him because of his connection with the Russian Church, and finding that the Serbian Orthodox Mission was then (as he said) "left without resources, aid and, what is more, goodwill,"[91] at the end of 1909 Fr. Sebastian asked Archbishop Platon to relieve him of his

[90] Bishop Sava, pp. 35, 42, 176–77.
[91] Fr. Sebastian Dabović to Archbishop Platon. Written in Oakland, California, December 6, 1909. Quoted in Bishop Sava, pp. 34–35.

duties as administrator of the Mission. At the same time he wrote a letter to the Holy Synod of Bishops in Serbia, informing them of the situation of the Serbian Orthodox churches in America and asking for their aid:

> Most Serbs have said that they do not want any other jurisdiction, not even Russian, but their own Serbian Church jurisdiction. On this day I am submitting to North American Archbishop Platon my resignation as administrator of the Serbian Mission, for I am exhausted from the effort and cannot oppose a multitude single-handed.... Once again I caution the Holy Synod that the Serbian Church in glorious, vast America has been left without an administrator and I urge that a Serbian archpastor be sent.[92]

Archbishop Platon reported to the Holy Synod of Bishops in Russia about Fr. Sebastian's request to resign. When the bishops in Russia sent back a Decision to Archbishop Platon granting Fr. Sebastian's request, they felt it necessary to recount the praise that St. Tikhon had given eight years earlier for Fr. Sebastian's accomplishments in America:

> Concerning the Hieromonk Sebastian, His Grace Tikhon of the Aleutians, in his communication to the Holy Synod of June 2, 1902, no. 74, wrote that the appointed Hieromonk, during his service in the Mission, exerted considerable efforts towards 1) building holy churches in America (the construction of churches in Jackson and Seattle, and the decoration of the cathedral church in San Francisco), 2) organizing church-parish life in Minneapolis shortly after the parishioners joined the Orthodox Church, 3) raising religious and national consciousness among Slavs scattered across America, 4) acquainting non-Slav Christians (primarily Episcopalians) in America with the teachings of the Orthodox Church, for which purpose he wrote and published, from his meager resources, several books in English, and 5) translating official documents of the Administration into English.[93]

---

[92] Fr. Sebastian Dabović to the Holy Hierarchical Synod, Karlovci Patriarchate. Written in Oakland, California, December 14, 1909. Quoted in Bishop Sava, p. 35.

[93] Decision no. 4822 of June 22, 1910, Archives of the Synod of the Russian Orthodox Church. Quoted in Bishop Sava, p. 36.

The St. Basil of Ostrog Church in Angels Camp,
California. Photo courtesy Andjelka Raicević.

"Go Ye Therefore, and Teach All Nations" (Matt. 28:19)

After being released from his position as head of the Serbian
Mission in 1910, Fr. Sebastian served the Serbian Orthodox communities in California. As he wrote to Archbishop Platon:

> The receipts from modest services performed for the many Serbs
> in the cities of Los Angeles, Fresno and Oakland, I hope, will be
> enough to nourish me. The new church in Angels Camp is al-
> ready finished, and to there and to the church in Jackson a new
> priest, Fr. Jovan Dučić, will soon be coming from Herzegovina.
>
> The mission in [Bisbee] Arizona has been reorganized into a
> parish, and Fr. Samuel Popović from the Timisoara Diocese will
> be coming to build a new church.[94]

[94] Fr. Sebastian Dabović to Archbishop Platon. Written in Oakland, California, December 6, 1909. Quoted in Bishop Sava, p. 35.

The Serbian church communities in these cities and towns had been organized by Fr. Sebastian himself. As mentioned earlier, Fr. Sebastian had begun to establish a parish in the mining town of Angels Camp during his early visits to Jackson, located only twenty-seven miles away. In 1909 the Serbian community in Angels Camp, numbering about 1,500 people, began building a church. The church was consecrated on August 14, 1910, and was dedicated to St. Basil of Ostrog.

Since the congregation in Angels Camp, together with

St. Sava Church, Los Angeles.

those in Jackson and Bisbee, were already being served by priests from Serbia, Fr. Sebastian now settled among the Serbian congregation he had organized in Los Angeles, while paying regular pastoral visits to the smaller communities in Oakland and Fresno.[95] Under his leadership, in 1909 the Los Angeles congregation purchased a large plot of land on the east side of the city for use as a cemetery, and began building a church on this land. Fr. Sebastian held services in a temporary home chapel while the church's construction was underway. In 1911 the completed church was consecrated by Fr. Sebastian in honor of St. Sava of Serbia.[96]

In 1912 the Balkan Wars broke out, and Fr. Sebastian felt called to help his suffering Serbian brothers. As the *Los Angeles Times* reported:

---

[95] Serbian Orthodox churches were eventually consecrated in Oakland and Fresno, in 1926 and 1957 respectively.

[96] This church building served the Serbian community until 1963, when the new St. Sava Church was built in San Gabriel. The old church still stands, surrounded by the Serbian Orthodox cemetery, and services are still held in it occasionally.

St. Platon's Orthodox Theological Seminary, Tenafly, New Jersey.

The Balkan War between the Serbs and Turks has developed many cases of self-sacrifice among the Serbs in and around Los Angeles, but probably none greater than that of Father Sebastian Dabovich... who for two years has been working among the Slavs and Greeks of this city, to induce them to higher ideals in living. He has built a small chapel on Boyle Heights and has just begun to get his work on a better footing, when he feels called upon to sacrifice his personal belongings for the benefit of the hospital work in the Serb army.[97]

Fr. Sebastian auctioned off all his valuable possessions for the medical treatment of wounded Serbian soldiers—including his archimandrite's mitre from Russia,[98] his jeweled pectoral cross from Serbia, his handpainted icons, all his awards and decorations from foreign dignitaries, and a handmade rug from Macedonia.[99]

Even the sacrifice of his small number of treasured possessions was not enough for him; he wanted to do more. Thus, although he had hoped to stay at the St. Sava Church in Los Angeles as the resi-

[97] "Patriotic Sacrifice," *Los Angeles Times,* October 25, 1912, p. II-9.
[98] Evidently this mitre was different from the above-mentioned mitre given him by St. Tikhon.
[99] Ibid.

dent priest, he left this position and returned to Serbia in order to serve as a chaplain in the Serbian army.

The trip lasted the better part of a year. During this time, Fr. Sebastian took the opportunity to make a pilgrimage to the holy places in Kosovo and the other Serbian Orthodox lands. While in Belgrade, as an American citizen he was invited to officiate at the United States Consulate for Thanksgiving Day services.

When visiting Skopje, Fr. Sebastian wrote a letter to Nikola Pašić, President of the Ministry of Foreign Affairs in Belgrade, in which he expressed his hope that a Serbian diocese would finally be created in America, with a Serbian bishop residing there. It is noteworthy that he named St. Nikolai (Velimirović) as a candidate for becoming the Serbian bishop for America at that early date, when St. Nikolai was still a hieromonk. As Fr. Sebastian wrote to Nikola Pašić, "You have two candidates in Serbia, Nikolai and Valerian.[100] I consider myself a third only if necessary."[101]

In August 1913, having returned to the United States, Fr. Sebastian visited San Francisco and spoke at an Episcopal Church there. When St. Platon's Orthodox Theological Seminary was established by Archbishop Platon in Tenafly, New Jersey that same year, he became one of its first instructors, bringing with him many years of experience of teaching in church schools. There he prepared for ordination several Serbian seminarians, who went on to become much-needed priests for the Serbian parishes in America.[102]

While based on the East Coast, Fr. Sebastian continued to travel to the Serbian parishes that were still without a priest, in order to serve the Divine Liturgy and pastor the faithful. These included not only parishes in the United States but also a parish in Canada: for a time he served at the Serbian Orthodox Church of St. Nicholas in Hamilton, Ontario, Canada, which was established in 1913.[103] He also continued to be involved in conferences and discussions with the non-Orthodox. Here he took the same charitable yet uncom-

---

[100] Hieromonk Valerijan (Boshnjaković).

[101] Fr. Sebastian Dabović to Nikola Pašić. Written in Skopje, November 20, 1912. Quoted in Bishop Sava, p. 49.

[102] Mirko Dobrijević (Bishop Irinej), p. 15.

[103] Bishop Sava, pp. 11, 18.

promising approach that he had always taken in witnessing Orthodoxy to the non-Orthodox, *speaking the truth in love.*

In 1915 Fr. Sebastian met with St. Nikolai (Velimirović), then an archimandrite, in San Francisco. As St. Nikolai later recalled, Fr. Sebastian met him at the train station, introduced him to many Serbs in the city, and took him to the Holy Trinity Cathedral. A close spiritual kinship developed between these two dedicated missionaries. St. Nikolai was later to describe Fr. Sebastian as follows:

The original St. Nicholas Church in Hamilton, Ontario.

> He was a sincere and convinced believer and a Christian missionary of world-scope. He traveled restlessly and preached and lectured indefatigably. He composed books, wrote articles, epistles, and thousands of private letters to laymen and priests with needed explanations, exhortations and encouragements. He spoke and wrote in Serbian, English, and Russian. His clumsy handbag was always full with New Testaments, religious booklets, printed sermons and tracts. Also with small crosses for boys and girls. All this he distributed freely. He never visited a Serbian family empty-handed. He remembered the apostolic words: *It is more blessed to give than to receive* (Acts 20:35).[104]

By this time all the chartered Serbian parishes in America had elected to leave the Russian Church and to place themselves under the hierarchy of the Serbian Church. The Russian Church did not agree to this, and tensions understandably ensued.[105] Fr. Sebastian managed to remain relatively uninvolved in the brewing conflict, but still he was not spared being subjected to unjust accusations.

---

[104] Bishop Nikolai (Velimirović), "Father Sebastian Dabovich."
[105] Bishop Sava, pp. 49–61.

Whereas formerly he had been resented by some Serbs for being too pro-Russian, now he was resented by some Russians for being too pro-Serbian. Archbishop Evdokim (Meschersky),[106] who as Archbishop Platon's replacement in America was trying to keep the Serbian parishes under Russian jurisdiction, accused Fr. Sebastian of "agitating against the Russian church authorities in America" and St. Nikolai (Velimirović) of "spreading dissension among Serbian parishes in America."[107] On October 5, 1916, Archbishop Evdokim called an Assembly of Serbian Clergy in Chicago, with the purpose of, as he said, "sorting out the ambitions of the Serbs."[108] At this meeting, presided over by the archbishop, Fr. Sebastian was roundly criticized. Afterwards Fr. Sebastian received a letter of sympathy from one of the Serbian priests present, Fr. Matej Stijačić:

> With a feeling of profound pain in my soul, I remembered long after our meeting in Chicago... that business of 'bearded children,'[109] and also the personal attacks on Your person at every opportunity. Believe me, the sympathies of the Serbian clergy were never so much on Your side as they are today.[110]

Contrary to what was being said about him, Fr. Sebastian's primary concern was not, as we have seen, the question of Russian or Serbian jurisdiction, but rather the proper shepherding of Christ's flock. As St. Nikolai wrote, Fr. Sebastian "never engaged in fruitless polemics"; and hence, during this period of controversy, he "went on with his apostolic mission all over America from coast to coast. Thus many times he visited lonely Serbian families in deserts and wildernesses to administer Holy Sacraments and bring consolation."[111]

---

[106] Archbishop Evdokim arrived in America in May 1915. He returned to Russia in August 1917, where in 1922 he became a metropolitan of the schismatic "Living Church."

[107] "Decree of His Imperial Highness, All-Russian Autocrat and the Host Governing Synod to Aleutian and North American Archbishop Evdokim," St. Petersburg, June 18, 1916. Quoting from "Archbishop Evdokim to the Most Holy Governing Synod," New York, June 15, 1915. Quoted in Bishop Sava, p. 56.

[108] "Svjedjenije" (Testimony), October 18, Archives of the American Orthodox Church. Quoted in Bishop Sava, p. 60.

[109] Evidently an accusation that Serbian priests, who had beards, were behaving like children.

[110] Priest Matej Stijačić to Archimandrite Sebastian. Written in Indiana Harbor, Indiana, November 15, 1916. Quoted in Bishop Sava, p. 184.

[111] Bishop Nikolai (Velimirović), "Father Sebastian Dabovich."

St. Nikolai (Velimirović) of Žiča (1880–1956)
during his early years as a bishop.

World War I was then raging, and Fr. Sebastian felt he could not neglect his suffering brethren in the Old Country. He asked the Holy Synod of the Russian Church to release him so that he could serve the Serbian Church in the land of his ancestors. In 1917 this request was granted, and Fr. Sebastian went to Serbia once again to serve as chaplain in the Serbian army.

After his return from Serbia, Fr. Sebastian again met St. Nikolai in America in February of 1921, this time in New York City. Two years earlier St. Nikolai had been consecrated as a bishop in Serbia, and his visit to America in 1921 marked the first time that any Serbian hierarch had come to the New World. Here is how St. Nikolai remembered his meeting with Fr. Sebastian during that trip:

His poverty amazed me when I met him... I invited him to lunch. Blushing, he said, "Thank you; I just bought a roll of bread with my last five cents." And salary? None. He lived on people's freely given donations. And still, even with empty pockets, he planned new journeys to Alaska, to Japan, and of course to Europe.

"But you are without means!" I remarked.

He smiled with his usual childlike and fascinating smile and quoted the Bible: *"The Lord will provide"* (cf. Gen. 22:8). And marvelously enough, the Lord always provided for His faithful servant.[112]

For his part, Fr. Sebastian saw in St. Nikolai a true man of God. Now that St. Nikolai was a bishop, Fr. Sebastian felt even more strongly that he was the best candidate to become the first Serbian Orthodox hierarch in America. By this time the tensions between the Russian Church and the Serbian Orthodox congregations in America had essentially ended, for with the Russian Revolution of 1917 a rupture had occurred in contacts between the Church in Russia and its American archdiocese. In 1921 the Greek Orthodox Archdiocese of America was established and was soon to receive its first Greek bishop.[113] St. Nikolai, meanwhile, had come to America with an assignment from the Holy Assembly of Bishops in Serbia to study the situation of the Serbian congregations in America and determine how they could be organized. Thus seeing greater hope that a Serbian hierarch could be consecrated for the Serbian flock in America, Fr. Sebastian wrote to Patriarch Dimitrije of Serbia on March 30, 1921:

> Considering the conditions and problems of the Serbian population in colonies across America, with their churches, organization and needs, it is imperative to undertake as soon as possible the reorganization and unification of our parishes and missions there, so that it truly becomes the Serbian Church in America. His Grace Bishop Nikolai could do this, taking advantage of the present circumstances which are well known to him, especially since he enjoys the sympathies of the authorities there. Asking

---

[112] Ibid.
[113] Bishop (later Archbishop) Alexander (Demoglou) of Rodostolon.

Your Holiness to confer the blessing in the form of assistance in the struggle for the Orthodox Church in America...[114]

On September 21, 1921, Metropolitan Varnava (the future Patriarch of Serbia) nominated St. Nikolai as Bishop of America, with Archimandrite Mardarije (Uskoković) as his administrative assistant. Many pious people in Serbia objected to the nomination of St. Nikolai, being unwilling to relinquish their beloved "New Chrysostom."[115] Thus, in 1923 Archimandrite Mardarije was appointed administrator of the newly formed Serbian Orthodox Diocese of North America and Canada. According to Fr. Mardarije, the hierarchy in Serbia "were thinking of electing as Bishop for the American Church one of the three archimandrites in America, and they are: Sebastian Dabović, Georgije Kodžić, both from California, and myself. Who will be chosen is a big question."[116] In its fall meeting of 1925, the Holy Assembly of Serbian Bishops elected Archimandrite Mardarije as the Bishop of the American-Canadian Diocese. On April 25, 1926, Fr. Mardarije was consecrated to the episcopacy in the Orthodox cathedral in Belgrade, and in July he arrived in his diocese as the first Serbian bishop of America.

His Final Years and Repose in Serbia

In the years following World War I, Fr. Sebastian traveled many times between America and Serbia, carrying on his untiring pastoral work. As St. Nikolai recorded, in 1921 Fr. Sebastian was "engaged by the American Bible Society to distribute Bibles in the Balkans."[117] In America, he continued to serve not only in Serbian Orthodox churches but also in the homes of believers who lived far from an Orthodox church or were unable to drive to one. One of these, An-

---

[114] Fr. Sebastian Dabović to Serbian Patriarch Dimitrije. Written in New York, March 30, 1921. Quoted in Bishop Sava, p. 86.

[115] Fr. Daniel Rogich, *Serbian Patericon,* vol. 1 (Platina, Calif.: St. Herman of Alaska Brotherhood, 1994), p. 234.

[116] Archimandrite Mardarije to Dr. Paja Radosavljević. Written in Chicago, Illinois, April 3, 1924. Quoted in Bishop Sava, pp. 109–10.

[117] "Report of Bishop Nikolai of Ohrid to the Holy Bishops' Assembly Concerning the Situation and Needs of the Serbian Orthodox Church in America," Sremski Karlovci, June 26, 1921. Quoted in Bishop Sava, p. 93.

na Smilanić, remembers Fr. Sebastian baptizing her as a child in 1926, in her family's home in Long Beach, California.[118]

Fr. Sebastian also made missionary journeys to the Orthodox Mission in Japan, which had long interested and inspired him. St. Nikolai of Žiča records that Fr. Sebastian, during his lifetime, crossed the Atlantic fifteen times and the Pacific nine times. He also writes that St. Nicholas of Japan, sometime before his repose in 1912, had offered Fr. Sebastian to stay in Japan and serve the Orthodox mission there.[119] Although Fr. Sebastian did not stay there permanently, he was able to visit the Japanese Mission many times, offering his wealth of pastoral experience.

Finally, when Fr. Sebastian crossed the Atlantic for the fifteenth time and came to Serbia, he stayed there until the end. Not long before his repose, his fellow Serbian priests in America wrote to the Patriarch of Serbia: "We take the liberty of mentioning that our Homeland has acknowledged the religious and national work of our elder brother, Archimandrite Sebastian Dabović, who is spending his old age in retirement."[120]

St. Nikolai of Žiča describes the last years of Fr. Sebastian's life as follows:

> Patriarch Varnava gave him an apartment in the Patriarchate, where he stayed until 1938. Then he moved to Žiča, where he stayed with us for some time, then again to Herceg Novi. On his way to and fro he was steadily accompanied by Rev. Jovan Rapaich, whom he loved most of all and who took true filial care of the old man. Finally he returned definitely to Žiča, his last resort. He stayed with us until the end of 1940. From there he wrote many letters to his American friends. In a letter to Mr. Niko Mussich he wrote: "My body is getting weaker and weaker. I would like to see once more the Golden Gate. All my dear-

---

[118] Anna was born in 1922 to Drago and Elena Vuksanović. She now lives in Fresno, California, where her son-in-law, Protopresbyter George Gligich, is the rector of the St. Peter Serbian Orthodox Church.

[119] Bishop Nikolai (Velimirović), "Father Sebastian Dabovich."

[120] "Statement/Appeal of the Priesthood of the Serbian Orthodox Church of the American-Canadian Diocese, Humbly Sent to His Holiness, Archbishop of Pech and Metropolitan of Belgrade and Karlovac, Dr. Gavrilo, Patriarch of Serbia." (This document is not dated; since His Holiness Gavrilo was elected patriarch in 1938 it would have been written during the last two years of Fr. Sebastian's life.) Quoted in Bishop Sava, p. 188.

Žiča Monastery in Serbia, where Archimandrite Sebastian reposed in 1940.
Photograph taken in 2006.

est memories from childhood are concentrated in San Francisco and in the country in which I was born."[121]

I visited him frequently, asking how the brothers served him. His heart was failing. Fr. Rapaich was with him day and night. The last time, on my return from the diocese, I went to see him. Sitting in an armchair, he was breathing heavily and spoke in a whisper.

"Do you have any wish, Father?" I asked.

"Only the Kingdom of Heaven."

He spoke no more. These were his last words, representative of his entire career on earth. After that he gave up his spirit. He died on November 30, 1940.

The next day he was buried in the monastery's cemetery alongside another famous archimandrite, Fr. Raphael, formerly the Superior of the great Serbian monastery Hilandar on the Holy Mountain, who died in Žiča in 1937. During the night the sea-

[121] Out of humility, St. Nikolai did not quote the sentence that follows, in which Fr. Sebastian writes: "I am thankful to His Grace Bishop Nikolai, who is doing all he can to restore my health." Quoted in *The Diocesan Observer,* no. 503 (December 24, 1975).

son's first snow covered the earth, and it was cold. Yet His Excellency the American Ambassador Arthur Bliss Lane sent the American Consul General from Belgrade to represent him at the burial. For Fr. Sebastian was an American citizen. Besides, Mr. Bliss Lane had great personal devotion to him, calling him "my spiritual father Dabovich."

So ended the earthly pilgrimage of a great servant of Christ and the greatest Serbian missionary of modern times. He was a missionary by words, by deeds, and—what is the greatest of all—by his personal character. He was a viceless man. Meek and unpretentious, he was positive and constructive in all his words and works. He never engaged in fruitless polemics. Externally he was a little, lean man, with a beard. Just the kind of priest the Serbian immigrants liked, remembering their bearded priests in the Old Country. And behold, he was American-born and not an immigrant. But his conviction was that an Orthodox priest ought to be recognizable as Orthodox by his exterior, too.[122]

Archimandrite Sebastian was buried in the cemetery of the Žiča Monastery. "At the time of his death," writes Bishop Irinej, "Fr. Sebastian owned nothing more than a gold cross, some books, and a few personal mementos. He had long since given away any significant personal possessions to the poor and needy, choosing for himself a life of poverty, simplicity, and dedicated missionary service."[123]

Ten years after Fr. Sebastian's repose, St. Nikolai wrote of him:

Here is a man who indebted all the Serbian race, especially all the Serbs and all the Serbian organizations in America. Should that man remain without a monument or any sign of honor on American soil? He does not need it. He did not wish it. All he wished to his last breath was the Kingdom of Heaven, which I believe he has obtained by the grace of his Lord. But his people need it; his posterity needs it. The Serbian people always cultivated the noble virtue of gratitude. Let them express their traditional gratitude to this remarkable Serbian—Father Sebastian Dabovich.[124]

---

122 Bishop Nikolai (Velimirović), "Father Sebastian Dabovich."
123 Mirko Dobrijević (Bishop Irinej), p. 13.
124 Bishop Nikolai (Velimirović), "Father Sebastian Dabovich."

With the transfer of Fr. Sebastian's relics from Serbia to America—to the first Serbian church in America, which he founded in Jackson, California—this outstanding missionary was shown, in his native country, the gratitude of which he was worthy. He sacrificed himself unremittingly for Christ's Holy Church throughout America and the world, creating new churches where they were needed, and spiritually strengthening those that already existed. It was his tremendous love for Jesus Christ and His Church that not only inspired but *drove* him in his apostolic ministry, that made him burn with zeal as he labored to bring all peoples into the fullness of the Church's grace. We are the inheritors of his spiritual legacy in America—the legacy of a life given wholly to Christ.

Even as Fr. Sebastian was being appropriately honored in America, the story of his righteous life and apostolic labors was being spread among the people of Serbia. Now, with the decision of the Holy Assembly of Bishops of the Serbian Orthodox Church to enter Archimandrite Sebastian into the Calendar of Saints—together with that of Bishop Mardarije (Uskoković), another Serb of holy life who labored selflessly in America—this humble servant of God is glorified as a saint of the universal Orthodox Church. As St. Sebastian's missionary work continues to bear fruit in the many parishes he founded, helped to establish, and served in, may his example inspire new generations of Orthodox Christians to share and spread their precious Faith. Expressing their gratitude to St. Sebastian and calling upon him in the Kingdom of Heaven, believers will find in him a fervent intercessor, caring for God's people with the same love that drove him during his earthly sojourn. Holy Father Sebastian, Apostle of Christ, pray to God for us!

✳ ✳ ✳
Kontakion
to Saint Sebastian of Jackson,
Tone 8:

Born in San Francisco,
Apostle and Enlightener of America,
The first American-born priest,
A fiery preacher of the word of Christ
    among the peoples of America:
You traveled across the entire country preaching
    the Truth in Love,
Establishing a multitude of souls in the Orthodox faith,
And erecting many churches to the glory of God,
Poor in body, but rich in Spirit.
Pray now to the Lord, Whom you served with all your heart,
O Sebastian, the Apostle of Jackson and All America,
That He may grant us your last spoken desire:
The Kingdom of Heaven, which has no end.

Map of Saint Sebastian's pastoral and missionary activity in North America

Archimandrite Sebastian Dabović

(Helpful information for making a map of important places in his life.)

1. **Saint Sebastian founded the following parishes** (by organizing, supporting and encouraging the local Orthodox Christian faithful):
Saint Nicholas Church in Portland, Oregon
Saint Spyridon Cathedral in Seattle, Washington
Holy Trinity Church in Wilkeson, Washington
Saint Sava Church in Jackson, California
Holy Trinity Church in Butte, Montana
Saint Basil of Ostrog Church in Angels Camp, California
Saint Sava Church in Los Angeles, California
Holy Resurrection Cathedral in Chicago, Illinois
Saint Sava Church in Douglas, Alaska (Bishop Sava mentions priest Aleksandar Jarošević as the founder; Fr. Sebastian was administrating the Alaskan Deanery at the time when the church was built, so he undoubtedly closely oversaw the progress and took part in the consecration.)

2. **Saint Sebastian served the following**, still existing and active, **parishes**:
Saint Basil Cathedral in San Francisco, Ca (now Holy Trinity Cathedral)
Saint Mary's Cathedral in Minneapolis, Minnesota
Holy Transfiguration Cathedral in Denver, Colorado
Saint Nicholas Cathedral in Hamilton, Ontario (Canada)

3. **Saint Sebastian contributed to founding the following parishes** (by making initial pastoral contacts with the local Orthodox Christians, who later on founded the parishes):
St. Peter the Apostle Church in Fresno, California
St. George Church in Oakland, California
St. Stephen Nemanja Church in Bisbee, Arizona
St. Nicholas Church in Juneau, Alaska
(There are probably others as well, which future research studies will hopefully discover.)

4. **Saint Sebastian participated in consecrating the following churches**:
Saint Sava Church in Jackson, California
Saint Sava Church in Douglas, Alaska
Holy Trinity Cathedral in San Francisco, California
Saint Nicholas Church in Wilmerding, Pennsylvania
Saint George Church in Indiana Harbor, Indiana (second consecration)

5. **Saint Sebastian taught in the following schools**:
Church School of Saint Basil Cathedral in San Francisco, California
Missionary School of Saint Mary's Church in Minneapolis, Minnesota
Saint Platon's Orthodox Theological Seminary in Tenafly, New Jersey

The Translation of Archimandrite Sebastian's Relics from Serbia to America

by Hieromonk Damascene (Christensen)

SEPTEMBER 1, 2007, marked a celebration of great significance for Orthodoxy in America, when the relics of Archimandrite Sebastian Dabović were interred in the St. Sava Church in Jackson, California. The first of many churches founded by Fr. Sebastian (in 1894), the St. Sava Church is the oldest Serbian Orthodox church in the Western Hemisphere.

The interment of Fr. Sebastian's remains in this historic church was preceded by their transfer from the other side of the world. Having been born in San Francisco and having labored for most of his life as a missionary throughout the United States, Fr. Sebastian spent his last years in his ancestral land of Serbia, where he reposed in Žiča Monastery on November 30, 1940. After Fr. Sebastian's body was buried in the snow-covered ground of the Žiča cemetery by his spiritual friend and fellow missionary St. Nikolai (Velimirović) of Žiča, his grave was marked by a simple cross.

In the sixty-seven years that have passed since Fr. Sebastian's repose, veneration for him by Orthodox Christians has taken root and grown. An impetus toward this veneration came on the tenth anniversary of his repose, when St. Nikolai of Žiča, then living in America, gave a beautiful speech on Fr. Sebastian's many accomplishments and virtues, calling his fellow Serbs to honor the memory of this modern-day apostle.[1]

After St. Nikolai, one of the first Orthodox writers to recognize and make known Fr. Sebastian's greatness was the co-editor of *The*

---

[1] Bishop Nikolai (Velimirović), "Father Sebastian Dabovich," in *Serb National Federation Commemorative Book, 1951.*

Orthodox Word, Fr. Seraphim (then Eugene) Rose. In 1965, the twenty-fifth anniversary of Fr. Sebastian's repose and the first year of *The Orthodox Word's* publication, Fr. Seraphim wrote and printed an article on Fr. Sebastian, followed by a chapter, "The True Church of Christ," from one of Fr. Sebastian's books.[2] In his article, Fr. Seraphim wrote: "Few Orthodox Americans are perhaps aware of the promising beginning of the Orthodox mission in the eighteenth and nineteenth centuries, when a serious attempt was undertaken to make the riches of Holy Orthodoxy accessible to Americans. One of the most notable examples—and results—of this missionary endeavor was the life and writings of Archimandrite Sebastian Dabovich."[3] Years later, in talking about the beginning of American Orthodox missionary work in the English language in the early part of the twentieth century, Fr. Seraphim called Archimandrite Sebastian "the outstanding Orthodox missionary" of that period.[4]

Over the years, articles and books on the history of Orthodoxy in America devoted special attention to Fr. Sebastian and his far-reaching influence. The many Serbian churches he founded or served in, as well as many non-Serbian ones, remembered with gratitude his pioneering missionary labors in America. Back in Serbia, however, Fr. Sebastian remained relatively unknown. The primary place of his apostolic work—the United States—was far away from the land where he had reposed and been laid to rest; and the Communist takeover of Serbia six years after his repose hindered contact between the two countries. By the 1980s, nothing was known about him at his resting place in Žiča Monastery, beyond the fact that he had been born in America.

At this time, another American-born Serb, Mirko Dobrijević— the future Bishop Irinej of the Serbian Orthodox Diocese of Aus-

---

[2] Archimandrite Sebastian Dabovich, "The True Church of Christ," *The Orthodox Word,* no. 5 (1965), pp. 182–87. The following year, two other articles by Fr. Sebastian were published in *The Orthodox Word:* "The Sunday of Orthodoxy" (no. 7, pp. 20–23), and "O Joyful Light" (no. 10, pp. 129–32).

[3] [Eugene Rose], "Archimandrite Sebastian Dabovich and the Orthodox Mission to America, *The Orthodox Word,* no. 5 (1965), p. 181.

[4] Hieromonk Seraphim Rose, "Orthodoxy in the USA: Its Historical Past and Present [a talk delivered at the St. Herman Winter Pilgrimage, Dec. 12/25, 1979, Holy Trinity Monastery, Jordanville, N.Y.], *The Orthodox Word,* no. 94 (1980), p. 212.

tralia and New Zealand—began to research Fr. Sebastian's life. The more Mirko learned about Fr. Sebastian, the more he became inspired by his life and witness, and the more he came to love and revere him as a holy man of God.

In 1984 Mirko went to Fr. Sebastian's resting place in Žiča for the first time. "When I came to his grave," recalls the now Bishop Irinej, "I was heartbroken. There were, literally, two rusted metal bars wired together in the form of a cross, with his name partially preserved: ARCHIM. SEBASTIAN. Nothing more. Though I knew that this was in keeping with his humble and austere way of life, I felt that he deserved far more from us who now reap the benefits of his apostolic labors. I then asked the late Bishop Stefan of Žiča in 1986/7 for permission to solicit funds for a proper marker on his grave. I collected funds from parishioners at Holy Resurrection Cathedral in Chicago, which Fr. Sebastian had founded (I was then the Director of Christian Education at the cathedral); and I placed an article in *American Srbobran* and *The Path of Orthodoxy*, entitled 'Marking the Grave of Fr. Sebastian.' At this point some of his family stepped forward with donations.

"Enough money was collected to erect the gravestone. Bishop Stefan gratefully added the epitaph: 'The First American Serbian Orthodox Apostle.'"[5]

Soon afterward, iconographic renderings of Fr. Sebastian began to adorn the walls of Serbian Orthodox churches in America. In 1988, when Leonidas Diamontopoulos was commissioned to fresco the interior of the Holy Resurrection Cathedral in Chicago, the future Bishop Irinej sketched out iconographic renderings of Bishop Nikolai Velimirović and Fr. Justin Popović to be placed to the right of the iconostasis, and of Bishop Mardarije (the first Serbian Orthodox bishop of America) and Fr. Sebastian to be placed to the left. In subsequent years iconographic frescos of Fr. Sebastian, based on the same original sketch, were painted by Fr. Theodore Jurewicz on the walls of the church at New Gracanica Monastery in Grayslake, Illinois, and by Miloje Milinkovic on the walls of four churches: St. Sava Church in Libertyville, Illinois; St. George Church in Scher-

---

[5] Bishop Irinej of Australia and New Zealand to the author, Sept. 11, 2007.

erville, Indiana; Holy Assumption Church in Sacramento, California; and St. Sava Church in Jackson, California.

At St. Sava Church in Jackson, Fr. Sebastian had never been forgotten. The parishioners had erected a marble monument to Fr. Sebastian in their cemetery, and for years they had cherished the hope that he would be "brought back" to them—that his remains would rest at the first church he founded in America.

One parishioner in particular, Deacon Triva Pavlov, took the initiative in turning this wish into reality. In 2006 he received the support of the newly enthroned bishop of the Serbian Orthodox Diocese of Western America, His Grace Bishop Maxim. In January of 2007 Bishop Maxim sent a letter to His Grace Bishop Hrizostom of the Diocese of Žiča in Serbia,[6] requesting that Fr. Sebastian's remains be brought from Žiča to Jackson. This letter was sent along with a letter from the clergy and the parish council president of the Jackson parish, stating the same request.[7] The matter was presented by Bishop Hrizostom at the Holy Assembly of Bishops of the Serbian Orthodox Church in Belgrade, and the request was granted. Bishop Hrizostom then wrote to Bishop Maxim:

"Your Grace, in connection with the February 13/26, 2007 resolution, no. 145/section 94, of the Holy Synod of Bishops of the Serbian Orthodox Church, as a result of Your January 25, 2007 letter, E. no. 41, and the request of the St. Sava church-school parish of Jackson, California, we give Our Archpastoral blessing and approval that the bodily remains of Archimandrite Sebastian Dabović be transferred from Žiča Monastery to the church of St. Sava in Jackson. Your Grace's brother in Christ and co-worker—Bishop Hrizostom of Žiča."

News of Fr. Sebastian's return to America was greeted with joy by the Serbian Orthodox Diocese of Western America. Bishop Maxim set up a "Committee for the organization of the transfer and welcome of Archimandrite Sebastian," which prepared for the re-

---

[6] Bishop Hrizostom had served as the Bishop of the Serbian Orthodox Diocese of Western America from 1988 to 1992.

[7] The letter of request was signed by Protopresbyter Stavrofor Miladin Garić (the senior priest in Jackson, ordained to the priesthood by St. John of Shanghai and San Francisco), Priest Stephen Tumbas, Deacon Triva Pavlov, and parish president Slavko Kostić.

ception of Fr. Sebastian's remains in America and for their interment in the St. Sava Church in Jackson. It was decided that the interment would take place in conjunction with the "Diocesan Days" gathering of the Serbian Diocese of Western America, which would take place on Labor Day Weekend at the St. Sava Mission in Jackson, a mile from the church.

On Saturday, August 4, 2007, Fr. Sebastian's remains were exhumed from their grave in Žiča Monastery. Before the exhumation, the Divine Liturgy was served in the thirteenth-century Žiča Monastery church. Archimandrite Gerasim of Žiča presided, with Protopresbyter Djurica Gordić concelebrating and two deacons assisting. Protopresbyter Djurica was visiting from America, where he serves at the St. John the Baptist Serbian Orthodox Cathedral in San Francisco. It was by God's Providence that this priest from Fr. Sebastian's birthplace and hometown in America was granted to be present in Žiča for the event of Fr. Sebastian's exhumation.

That day a gentle rain covered the earth. Following the Liturgy, the above-mentioned clergy, the nuns of Žiča Monastery, and assembled pilgrims ascended the hill above the monastery, where the monastic cemetery is located. There Fr. Sebastian had been buried, along with former Bishops of Žiča Stefan and Vasilije. After over two hours of digging, Fr. Sebastian's copper casket was unearthed and his bones were carefully taken from it. Immediately a *Parastos* (memorial service) was held for Fr. Sebastian in the cemetery chapel.

The relics of Fr. Sebastian were sent to America on the following Wednesday. They arrived at the see of the Serbian Diocese of Western America in Alhambra, California, where Bishop Maxim clothed them in priestly vestments. Then, a few weeks later, they were taken to Jackson, where they were placed in a beautiful hardwood ossuary. During the preceding weeks, the ossuary had been lovingly made by Paul Sharp of the St. Gabriel Antiochian Orthodox Mission in the nearby town of Angels Camp—one of the many towns originally evangelized by Fr. Sebastian.

On Saturday, September 1, six hierarchs, thirty priests, six deacons, and numerous faithful gathered at the St. Sava Mission in Jackson to celebrate the transfer of Fr. Sebastian's relics from Serbia and their interment in the St. Sava Church. In the morning, the os-

Grave of Archimandrite Sebastian at Žiča Monastery, Serbia, before the exhumation of his remains.

suary with the relics of Fr. Sebastian was met by the hierarchs, clergy and faithful in front of the Mission. It was carried in procession by three priests who now serve in parishes that Fr. Sebastian founded in the western United States over a century ago (in Jackson, Los Angeles, and Butte), and by one priest who serves in a city where the Orthodox community was first organized by Fr. Sebastian (Seattle).[8]

The hierarchical Divine Liturgy was then celebrated under a large canopy at the Mission. (The Liturgy was celebrated outdoors at the Mission because the large number of people could not be accommodated at the St. Sava Church.) The liturgical celebration was presided over by Metropolitan Christopher of Mid-Western America (Serbian Orthodox Church), with the concelebration of Metropolitan Joseph of the USA, Canada and Australia (Bulgarian Orthodox Church), Archbishop Kyrill of San Francicso and Western America (Russian Orthodox Church Outside of Russia), and the Serbian hierarchs Bishop Irinej of Australia and New Zealand, Bishop Porfirije of Jegar,[9] and Bishop Maxim of Western America. The assembled priests and deacons, who belonged to several different Orthodox jurisdictions in America, took part in the service as well. All the dioceses of the Serbian Church in the United States and Canada were represented by the clergy and the faithful in attendance.

---

[8] The priests were Priest Stephen Tumbas of the St. Sava Church in Jackson, California; Protopresbyter Stavrofor Petar Jovanović of the St. Sava parish in Los Angeles (San Gabriel); Priest Russell Radoicich of Holy Trinity Church in Butte, Montana; and Priest Ilija Balach of the St. Sava Church in Seattle, Washington.

[9] Bishop Porfirije was visiting from the ancient monastery of Kovilj, near Novi Sad in northern Serbia.

Memorial to Archimandrite Sebastian, with St. Sava's Church
in the background, Jackson, California.

With Bishop Maxim's blessing, during the Liturgy Deacon Triva Pavlov was elevated to the rank of protodeacon by Bishop Irinej. It was a fitting day for Deacon Triva's elevation, since, as we have seen, it had been through his initiative that the day's celebrations had been made possible.

At the conclusion of the Liturgy, a *Parastos* was served for Fr. Sebastian, with the blessing of *kolyva*.[10] His Eminence Metropolitan Christopher presided, censing Fr. Sebastian's ossuary as he read and sang the prayers; and the hierarchs, clergy, and faithful participated in the singing.

---

[10] *Kolyva:* a special dish made with boiled wheat, which is blessed and served at a memorial service.

Memorial to the founders of the St. Sava Church in Jackson, California.

Bishop Irinej then gave a moving sermon on the life of Fr. Sebastian. The sermon was spoken from the heart, without the aid of written notes. Hearing Bishop Irinej's inspired words, one could sense that this moment and this day were a prelude to Fr. Sebastian's formal glorification as a saint of the Church. It was a prelude worthy of the man whom it extolled.

Having greeted all those who had gathered, Bishop Irinej began by recalling Fr. Sebastian's humble burial in Žiča Monastery many years previously, where he had died with almost no possessions. "It was by all earthly standards and measures a pauper's funeral," His Grace said, and yet, "indeed in many ways it was the most regal of coronations. It was the ushering into the Kingdom of Heaven of a man born so long ago here in America."

At this point, Bishop Irinej ceased to address his audience and began to address Fr. Sebastian himself. In this he demonstrated that Fr. Sebastian, whose relics then lay in an ossuary in front of the iconostasis, was not dead but alive—that his immortal soul, having ascended to heaven to be with Christ and His saints, had been granted to be present with the faithful in Jackson that very day, even as his earthly remains awaited the General Resurrection.

Speaking alternately in English and Serbian, Bishop Irinej addressed Fr. Sebastian as follows: "Welcome, our holy and venerable

Father Sebastian! Welcome, O first Serbian child born here on this American continent! Welcome back, holy missionary, you who spread Christ's Gospel from one side of this continent to the other! Welcome, our holy and venerable father, you who have established the Serbian Orthodox Church here as her founding father during this past century! Welcome, holy father, you who disregarded yourself for the sake of spreading the Gospel of Him Who gave life, resurrection and hope to you and to us; you who spread the Gospel in far-off Japan, Russia, Serbia, but most of all to us here on this American continent...

"Welcome to your home... to this town of Jackson, where you built in the year 1894 this magnificent temple dedicated to the first Serbian saint and enlightener, Sava. And that temple still stands, and you yourself will be ushered in in full glory by the hierarchs, the clergy, and the faithful of our Church, to rest in that sanctuary which you have built with your own hands, that sanctuary which stands here in testimony to your apostolic endeavors and missionary zeal on this continent."

Still addressing his words directly to Fr. Sebastian, Bishop Irinej outlined some of the main events of his life. His Grace then called to mind two parallel manifestations of Divine Providence—that, whereas the relics of St. Nikolai of Žiča were brought from America to his birthplace in Lelić, Serbia (in 1991), so now the relics of Fr. Sebastian have made the opposite journey in having been brought to rest in his native state of California:

"It was Blessed Bishop Nikolai who laid you in the earth—the same earth from which you were taken and brought here to this your fatherland in America. And all according to God's marvelous Providence, that same saint, Bishop Nikolai, who was born in Serbia and was buried here in America, returned to Serbia to lie in Lelić Monastery, where he radiates his joyful presence to all who come to venerate and call upon him, and where he is a source of enlightenment to this very day to our Serbian people. In like manner, the Holy Synod of Bishops of the Serbian Orthodox Church have deigned to return you, Fr. Sebastian, so that you will be a luminary here in Jackson, California, as St. Nikolai is in Lelić. Your teachings, your legacy, your life, all that you did for us will continue to glow

Procession to the site of the outdoor Divine Liturgy, St. Sava Mission, Jackson, California, September 1, 2007. The priests are carrying the ossuary with Fr. Sebastian's relics, followed by the hierarchs.

and to radiate from your presence here among us. You are by all standards, as Bishop Nikolai wrote of you, the greatest missionary of the Serbian Orthodox Church in this past century....

"And now you, holy Father Sebastian, freed from all earthly constraints, again live and abide here among us. Teach us, holy Father Sebastian, to be missionaries as you were! Teach us, holy Father Sebastian, to give up all that we treasure, all that binds and fetters us to this earth, so that we too may find the same apostolic wings that you possessed, so that we, as you, may help spread—each according to his ability and the gifts which have been bestowed upon him—the Gospel and the teachings of our Lord, God and Savior Jesus Christ. Welcome home, our holy and venerable Father Sebastian. Pray to God for us, your sinful kinsmen. Holy Father Sebastian, as we pray for you, pray for us before the throne of the Lord, before Whom you now stand in glory. Amen."

Having thus finished his words to Fr. Sebastian, Bishop Irinej again addressed the assembled faithful, saying, "May God grant the day of his illumination and glorification to come! Until that very day, may the Lord God be with us. Thank you, and God be

Parastos (memorial service) for Fr. Sebastian with the blessing of kolyva,
led by Metropolitan Christopher after the Divine Liturgy.

Metropolitan Christopher censing the relics of Fr. Sebastian
during the *Parastos*.

Metropolitan Christopher
giving the dismissal blessing at the end of the *Parastos*.
Hierarchs left to right: Bishop Maxim, Archbishop Kyrill, Metropolitan
Christopher, Metropolitan Joseph, Bishop Irinej, Bishop Porfirije.

Bishop Irinej giving a sermon on the life of Fr. Sebastian.

with you until we meet again in His Kingdom which will know no end. Amen."

At the conclusion of Bishop Irinej's sermon, Bishop Maxim went to the opened ossuary and placed an archimandrite's pectoral cross on Fr. Sebastian's relics. He then poured wine, according to tradition, on the vestments that covered the remains.

The hierarchs came up to venerate the relics, followed by the clergy and faithful. Each person was given a card with an icono-graphic rendering of Fr. Sebastian from the church of St. Sava Monastery in Libertyville, Illinois. On the back of the card was printed a beautiful prayer written by Fr. Sebastian, from his sermon "Thoughts for Good Friday at the Passion and Burial of Christ."[11]

After the veneration by the faithful, the ossuary was placed in a hearse. A procession of cars followed the hearse through the historic town of Jackson, and soon arrived at the St. Sava Church. There the aforementioned four priests carried the ossuary up the steep steps from the road to the hilltop church, passing through the cemetery. Halfway up, they were met by Protodeacon Triva, who guided the ossuary into the church.

The ossuary was placed on the ambo. By this time the church was tightly packed with people. Metropolitan Christopher censed the relics and poured wine on the vestments that covered them for the second time. As he did so, everyone in the crowded church sang in unison *"Vechnaya Pamyat"* (Memory Eternal), so loudly and with such prayerful feeling that it seemed that the walls shook.

The ossuary was then placed in a waterproof concrete vault that had been constructed beneath the floor on the right side of the church. As the priests were slowly lowering the ossuary into the vault, suddenly and spontaneously everyone broke into singing the Paschal troparion, "Christ Is Risen." The troparion was sung in both Slavonic and English, and again it was poured forth with such feeling that the voices reverberated from the walls. "It was the most spiritually uplifting moment of my life," Protodeacon Triva now recalls. With their heartfelt singing, the faithful were proclaiming that, because of

---

[11] Published in Fr. Sebastian Dabovich, *Preaching in the Russian Church* (San Francisco, 1899), pp. 131–32.

Christ's victory over death, His faithful servant Fr. Sebastian now *lived,* and would live forever in God. This, Christ's "trampling down death by death," was the central point of the very Gospel that Fr. Sebastian had devoted his life to preaching and spreading, thus enabling countless others to gain eternal life in Christ as well.

When the ossuary had been placed in the vault, a concrete lid was placed over the vault, and on top of it was placed a marble headstone. On the headstone were inscribed the words that had been previously written on Fr. Sebastian's gravestone in Žiča: "The First American Serbian Orthodox Apostle." At the bottom of the new headstone were added words anticipating Fr. Sebastian's listing in the Calendar of Saints: "Holy Apostle Sebastian, pray for us!"

Behind the headstone had been placed a large, upright, hardwood "prayer box," also made by Paul Sharp. On the front of it was inscribed a verse from the Epistle of St. Paul to the Ephesians which Fr. Sebastian had taken as his motto in his missionary labors: "Speak the Truth in Love" (cf. Eph. 4:15). Below that was a verse from the Psalms of David: "Precious in the sight of the Lord is the death of His Saints" (Ps. 115:6). In the conviction that Fr. Sebastian is indeed among the saints, a slot was made in the top of the hardwood box, so that the faithful could put in it written requests for Fr. Sebastian's heavenly intercessions.

The site of Fr. Sebastian's relics in the St. Sava Church in Jackson is now a place of pilgrimage for Orthodox Christians throughout America and the world. Together with the relics, the church treasures the miracle-working "Jackson Icon of the Mother of God," which was donated by the church's first hierarch, Bishop Nicholas (Ziorov) around the time of its consecration.

The interment of Fr. Sebastian's remains within the walls of the St. Sava Church, and the spiritual celebration that surrounded it, was a step toward a yet-more-joyous celebration: the glorification of Fr. Sebastian as a saint of the Orthodox Church. On May 29, 2015, the Holy Assembly of Hierarchs of the Serbian Orthodox Church added the name of Archimandrite Sebastian—together with that of Bishop Mardarije (Uskoković) of Libertyville—to the Calendar of Saints of the Orthodox Church; and on September 5, 2015, the Western American Diocese of the Serbian Orthodox Church plans

Metropolitan Christopher censing the ossuary with the relics of Fr. Sebastian,
after it had been placed on the ambo of the St. Sava Church,
Jackson, California.

to celebrate the public and liturgical glorification of the new saints
at St. Steven's Cathedral in Alhambra, California.

Notes on the Veneration of Righteous Ones:

Bishop Irinej of Australia and New Zealand has noted that veneration of righteous ones in the Church proceeds from God's revelation: "God reveals the sanctity of the person's life, which evolves
into local veneration by the faithful. In turn, that which God has
revealed is crowned by the Church with a formal proclamation of
glorification."

Bishop Maxim of Western America writes concerning the veneration of righteous ones before their formal glorification: "In the
Orthodox Church, veneration for a holy person is initiated by the
pleroma of the Church—the clergy and the faithful. Usually veneration entails a concurrence of local respect and synodal recognition. Sometimes the faithful begin to ask the holy person's intercessions on the local level, and later Orthodox hierarchs, based on what
the people of God have already proclaimed through this veneration,
make a conciliar decision to enter the name of the holy person in

The headstone and "prayer box" that were placed over the vault containing
Fr. Sebastian's relics. St. Sava Church, Jackson.
Photo by Victoria Stojanović.

St. Sava Church, Jackson, California.
Photo taken in 2005 by Victoria Stojanović.

the Calendar of Saints (which is the Orthodox tradition)—an act commonly known as 'canonization' or 'glorification.' Before the canonization, the Church does not celebrate services in honor of the holy person. Not infrequently, however, the faithful ask that person's heavenly intercessions, paint 'pre-canonization' iconographic portraits of him, and in some cases even call him 'saint' (which means 'holy'). Such was the case with St. Nikolai of Žiča, who was called 'saint' by the faithful long before his name was entered into the Calendar of Saints by the Holy Assembly of Serbian Orthodox Bishops in 2003."

St. Sava Church, Jackson, California.

Iconographic renderings of Fr. Sebastian. Above left: fresco by Leonidas Diamontopoulos, Holy Resurrection Cathedral, Chicago. Above right: fresco by Miloje Milinković, St. Sava Church, Libertyville, Illinois (Fr. Sebastian is shown holding St. Sava Church in Jackson, California). At bottom: fresco by Fr. Theodore Jurewicz, New Gracanica Monastery, Grayslake, Illinois.

III
Selected Writings

ЕП АМЕРИЧКО КАНАДСКИ МАРДАРИЈЕ УСКОКОВИЋ

St. Mardarije of Libertyville (1889–1935).
Commemorated November 29/December 12.

17ᵗʰ Archpastoral Epistle
of Bishop Mardarije
Pascha 1933

Mardarije, by God's grace Bishop of the Serbian Orthodox Diocese of America and Canada, upon his return from Yugoslavia sends from New York his archpastoral blessing to his dear fellow workers—priests and beloved Serbian people in his God-protected Diocese and greets everybody with the greeting:

Christ is Risen!

My dear brethren and my beloved flock,

On the third day after the Crucifixion of Christ, in the morning, two of his disciples, Luke and Cleopas, were travelling from Jerusalem to the nearby village of Emmaus. Along the way they spoke only of one thing—of the terrible event that had occurred three days before in the royal city of Jerusalem—the crucifixion of their Teacher and Lord Christ. With sad heart they retold everything that they had heard from him and observed over the three years. They marveled at how the harsh people could kill Him, Who during His entire lifetime had done nothing but good to people, Him Who was pure love and goodness. At the same time, they were anxious for themselves, for their lives, for the fate of the teachings of their beloved Teacher, feeling that they would be safer in their village than in Jerusalem, which was aflame with the malice of human passions and fearful human wrath.

Unexpectedly and inexplicably, there appeared suddenly, unnoticed, an unknown Traveler Who silently joined them on their journey and in their conversation along this desolate road. He walked alongside them for a long time, *but their eyes were restrained, so that they did not know Him* (Luke 24:16). The Traveler suddenly spoke in the language in which Luke and Cleopas were conversing and he asked them: *What kind of conversation is this that you have with one another as you walk and are sad?* Cleopas answered him: *Are You only a stranger in Jerusalem, and have You not known the things which happened there in these days?* And they told him how the chief priests and the rulers had condemned their teacher to death and crucified him in Jerusalem, and now it was the third day since he had been in the grave, *but we were hoping that it was He who was going to redeem Israel.*

> *Then He said to them, "O foolish ones, and slow of heart to believe in all that the prophets have spoken!... Ought not the Christ to have suffered these things and to enter into His glory?" Then they drew near to the village where they were going, and He indicated that He would have gone farther. But they constrained Him, saying, "Abide with us, for it is toward evening, and the day is far spent." And He went in to stay with them. Now it came to pass, as He sat at the table with them, that He took bread, blessed and broke it, and gave it to them. Then their eyes were opened and they knew Him; and He vanished from their sight. And they said to one another, "Did not our heart burn within us while He talked with us on the road, and while He opened the Scriptures to us?" So they rose up that very hour and returned to Jerusalem, and found the eleven and those who were with them gathered together, saying, "The Lord is risen indeed, and has appeared to Simon!" And they told about the things that had happened on the road, and how He was known to them in the breaking of bread. Now as they said these things, Jesus Himself stood in the midst of them, and said to them, "Peace to you"* (Luke 24:13-36).

And thus, my dear brethren, the disciples of Christ, Luke and Cleopas, saw on this day the resurrected Lord Christ and rushed from Emmaus back to Jerusalem to tell this joyful news to the others among their friends, the Apostles. One of the two, Luke, described this event in his Gospel, and I tell it to you as he wrote it down in the pages of that eternal book.

In this paschal epistle, I would like, my dear spiritual flock, to turn your attention especially to one place in that short story that was quoted above: "But their eyes were restrained, so that they did not know him."

Today's modern mankind has deluded itself into thinking that it will solve the heaviest and most complicated problems of life. They assemble themselves, represented by their most distinguished leaders and representatives, at numerous conferences. From all ends of the earth representatives come to these assemblies, and their paths take them to different cities. Alongside them, just like with Luke and Cleopas, Christ tries to join them, wants to travel with them and take part in these fateful meetings and assemblies for humanity. But, *their eyes are restrained, so that they do not know Him*, and this is the reason why those conferences never bear fruit. Even if they did accomplish something someday, this would all be provisional and it would be like the Gospel story of building a tower on sand. I do categorically believe that this is so, because I believe the words of Christ, Who said to people: *Without Me ye can do nothing* (John 15:5). As long as individuals and the entire humanity do not accept Christ as Luke and Cleopas accepted Him to eat with them, and as long as they do not believe that He is the Lord and their Leader, their eyes will not be open and they will not exit the darkness, which has enveloped them so thickly. Without Him they will wander around like a ship without a helm or a compass around the stormy sea of life. Without Christ a terrible shipwreck awaits humanity. Individuals and the entire humanity will see far worse days, and blessings and happiness will fly away from humanity as a bird flies away from its abandoned nest. *Your house is left to you desolate*, (Matt. 23:38; Luke 13:35), said the Lord.

This is why the Holy Church of Christ today raises its voice even though few hear it, and warns the nations to walk on the only way of salvation, on the path which leads to a complete and full solution of all possible problems and complications, on the path of Christ. "Your paths, O people, are false and insecure and they lead to death. Take for your guide Him to Whom all the paths and all the ways of the world are well-known, because He is the One Who said, *I am the Way, and the Truth, and the Life* (John 14:6)."

There was a man once who was travelling toward a city and he got lost and wandered off into the woods, and as he kept going the more lost he was. He wandered around for days. Having spent days in the woods without bread or water, he did not want to leave his bones there. But then he suddenly heard from afar the voice of a shepherd who was calling his flock. Overfilled with joy that he heard a human voice, this traveler, exhausted and with his clothes torn up already, turned in the direction where the voice came from, ran to the shepherd and asked him: "Which way do I go to reach the city?" And the shepherd mercifully took the traveler who was lost, brought him out of the woods and set him on the path which leads to the city.

You brothers, and you people, and all of humanity, all of you, take this one Shepherd and Guide—Christ—because He is the only one capable of leading us out of the forest of illusions, problems, intrigues, starvation, and death. If you do not do this, when even worse misfortune falls upon you and when you lose everything, don't crack the roof of the heavens with your painful, soul-splitting cries: "My God, my God, why have You forsaken me?" Do not blaspheme God, because your words are a terrible blasphemy and a mortal sin against eternal Truth and Justice, against the Holy Spirit. And it was said in the Holy Scripture: every sin will be forgiven to man, except the blasphemy against the Holy Spirit (cf. Mat. 12:31). And if you say such words, you are blaspheming against the Holy Spirit, against the eternal Justice and Truth, because God did not abandon you, but you are the one who abandoned God. So if you desire and are resolved to forsake God, then be a man and be a hero even in the hardest of circumstances and deprivations and even in the face of death itself, which is horrible without God. Be chivalrous, and instead of saying: "My God, my God, why have You forsaken me?" say openly and sincerely: "My God, my God, why have I forsaken You?"

Say it, O humanity! Say those salvific words already! And Christ will come to you, because He will hear your voice! Because He knows and hears everything, He awaits your voice, because He said: "Behold, I stand at the door of your heart and knock for you to open. And he who hears My voice, I will come in to him." (Rev. 3:20). And with Christ, you, O man, will exit the forest of illusions, lies and death and will walk on the path of eternal truth, justice, and life.

The corruption in the world today is assuming greater and greater proportions in all levels of the society and is endangering human civilization. People, even the most educated ones, refuse to see the destiny of the nations and humanity, which they have imposed upon themselves, that this monster of our age cannot be stopped and far less cured without Christ. O people, allow Him into the temple of your hearts, and He with His almighty right hand will drive out of your sanctuaries all those merchants as He once drove them out of the temple in Jerusalem. Without Christ, the world will suffocate in the sea of evil, envy, hatred, and wars of everybody against everybody, and the only people who will have any success will be those who have no principles.

Without Christ, nation will rise against nation, class against class, brother against brother, children against parents, and in the world mistrust and immorality will reign even more and they will not spare even the most sacred places, churches or courts, those holy of holies for humanity. And then the time will come, which was seen in a vision by the genius from Lovćen [Bishop and ruler of Montenegro Petar II Petrović Njegoš, one of the greatest poets of Serbian literature]: "My world has turned to hades and all people are ghosts from hell... Everything is going down the devil's path." Honesty and decency, character and friendship are gone, those things of which our ancestors boasted, and their offspring declares those same virtues now to be anachronism.

But great is the faith in our people, in their healthy souls, which will find its way out of this societal epidemic of today and will come out on the other end victorious, as we always have with faith in God throughout our painful history. Evil will not defeat our good people and, in our great Slavic family, a great mission awaits us. This mission is composed of becoming Christ-like and making the world Christ-like. This is the mission of my Slavic people in this world.

In studying the New Testament of Christ, I saw only two places where Christ the Lord cried—once in Bethany and then in Jerusalem, in Gethsemane. The first time He cried over a man and the second time over humanity—in the first case for Lazarus, and in the second case for all people. And today? Today He cries every day, with a sorrowful heart, which nineteen centuries ago was pierced with a spear on the Cross at Golgotha for the salvation of mankind. He is watching how people are trying, without Him, to build for themselves and their offspring an eternal house of happiness—sad people and pointless labors of lost children who have turned away from their Father. One entire nation of 150 million, of our race and our blood [the Soviets—ed.], would like by force, by fire and sword, to bring happiness to mankind, by making the belly and material riches the main goal in life. But I will say to that people very dear to my heart what Dostoyevsky said in his Grand Inquisitor, "The mystery of man is not in simply living, but in what he is living for." My dear Slavic brethren, you are never going to manage to build a house of happiness for anybody on the bones and the torments of other people. This is against the eternal principles of justice and morals, without which a man is not a man but an animal. Here is what that genius son of yours, Dostoyevsky, said in the book through the mouth of Ivan Karamazov to the main character of *The Brothers Karamazov*—Alyosha: "Tell me yourself, I challenge you—answer: Imagine that you are creating a fabric of human destiny with the object of making men happy in the end, giving them peace and rest at last, but that it was essential and inevitable to torture to death only one tiny creature ... and to found that edifice on its unavenged tears. Would you consent to be the architect on those conditions? Tell me, and tell the truth!"—"No, I wouldn't consent," answered Alyosha. And with Alyosha, the same answer is given by a hundred million Russians. "And can you admit the idea that men for whom you are building it would agree to accept their happiness on the foundation of the unexpected blood of a little victim? And accepting it would remain happy forever?"—"No, I can't admit it."

This is the answer of the Slavic people, and in that answer the true Slavic soul is revealed. And one day that soul will speak to the whole world, and the whole world will be astonished at the deep, intuitive introspection of the soul of my great Slavic tribe. When many Western nations start to think that the ship of the Slavic hope has sunk and that they can resolve the destiny of the world without the Slavs, the soul of our Slavic tribe, seeing the shores of the salvation, will begin its historic role in the world. Faith delivered that nation through the Mongol yoke that lasted for many centuries. It will deliver it also through every other yoke, no matter what the name of it might be, the yoke of the Boyars [aristocrats], of the Krepostniks [serf owners], of capitalism, or of communism.

Today when faith has practically disappeared in the world, not only faith in God, but faith in general, faith in oneself, faith in fellow men—and it is clear that without faith there is no life, no creating, no permanent inspiration or self-sacrifice—I believe that from the chest of our young great Slavic tribe will come the restoration of faith in God, faith in men, faith in oneself, and along with that faith as a new dynamic force, and the entire humanity will be moved forward and prompted to build a true house of happiness for all people and all nations. With such hopes and such faith in my Slavic tribe of 200 million and their historic mission in the world, I greet all of you, my dear brethren in America and Canada, with a heartfelt and joyous exclamation:

Christ is Risen!

Your humble intercessor in the Risen Christ,
Mardarije, Bishop of America and Canada
New York, Pascha 1933

18th Archpastoral Epistle of Bishop Mardarije

Christmas 1933

*at Saint Sava Monastery,
Libertyville, Illinois, by Chicago*

Mardarije, by God's grace, Bishop of the Orthodox Diocese of America and Canada, congratulates his dear clergy and people of his God-given Diocese the joyful day of Nativity of our Lord Jesus Christ, and greets all of them around America and Canada with a warm fatherly greeting:

Christ is Born!

My dear Brethren,

Over the small and until then unknown town of Bethlehem, on this day, nineteen centuries ago, there was a song, a song which was destined to be heard in all the languages of all the peoples in all the parts of the world. Early this morning the choirs of heavenly angels sang: *Glory to God in the highest, and on earth peace, goodwill among men* (Luke 2:14). On this quiet and peaceful night humanity was fast asleep. The shepherds around Bethlehem were watching their herds. Frightened by the unusual heavenly light and the unusual song of the even more unusual angelic choir, they saw before them the leader of the angels, who said to them: *Do not be afraid, for behold, I bring you good tidings of great joy which will be to all people. For there is born to you this day in the city of David a Savior, who is Christ the Lord* (Luke 2:10-11). The greatest event in the history of the world—today the Son of God is born. God Himself descended from heaven to the earth. Heaven and earth were joined together. God came to save sinful humanity. Through His teachings He showed the lost people the way which they should follow. And even more, by His death on the Cross at Golgotha He redeemed the sins of humanity and opened the gates of heaven for anyone that believes in Him, *for whoever calls on the name of the Lord shall be saved* (Rom. 10:13)

Humanity passed through various temptations and delusions, but it seems that the peak of all temptations and delusions has been reached at our day and age. Under the weight of delusions the tired and exhausted people fall, most of them never able to get up again. Is God so harsh and merciless that he should send such a heavy cross, such a burden and such a yoke to mankind? No, brethren. That burden under whose weight the back of humanity is breaking is not a burden from God. It is the burden of men. That is why it is so heavy. The burden of Christ is light. Under His burden not one back has ever broken, or even bent. On the contrary, people who carry the burden of Christ walk through life upright, singing psalms of praise to their God. If anyone is cured of an illness and again becomes happy and content, everybody else asks him for the medicine so that they also might be healed. There are people even today who have replaced the weight of the burden of men with ease of the burden of Christ, and thus they have solved the problems of life. Ask them for the recipe of that miraculous cure. They will tell you happily. Someone said once: "The more you try to push your cross away from you, the heavier it becomes." Such is the cross of every human being, because it is the cross of men, and the Lord Christ exclaimed twenty centuries ago to the tired people:

> Come to Me, all you who labor and are heavy laden, and I will give you rest. Take My yoke upon you and learn from Me, for I am gentle and lowly in heart, and you will find rest for your souls. For My yoke is easy and My burden is light (Mat. 11:28).

The purpose of the Lord's coming to the earth was that God's Kingdom and His righteousness be established on the earth. People are called to work on this. Their reward for this is inheriting the Kingdom of Heaven. And what can be more important than inheriting the eternal Kingdom in the glory of the heavenly Father? What have you, my brethren, done during your life on this earth that the Kingdom of Heaven and His righteousness should be established here? But you want to participate in the Kingdom of Heaven. What right do you have to ask to harvest the field which you never sowed? How can you expect to sit down at the royal dining hall of your Master when you did not serve Him faithfully? How can you go to the bank to make a withdrawal of the money that you never deposited? With what right would you ask for your soul to take part in God's Kingdom, if during your earthly life you contributed nothing to have that Kingdom of God established on the earth? Great and immeasurable is God's mercy, which forgives delusions and sins of people, but I would like it if my people were among the first in the construction of God's Kingdom. Some enter the Kingdom in rags and some in royal garment, each one according to his labor. Oh, how I would wish that my people would enter the Kingdom of eternal glory in royal garments.

Brethren, do not allow the spirit of the time to scandalize you. Atheism raises its head. The Church is suppressed as if it were done playing its role. Many will be scandalized and will fall away from her, thinking that she is finished. Do not be afraid—the Church is eternal, because God Who founded her is eternal. God suffers the sinners in order for the righteous to be manifested. God is slow but reachable, as the wise saying of our people says. Woe unto him who quarrels with his Creator (cf. Is. 45:9). If you do not want to be God's children, *God is able to raise up children to Abraham from these stones* (Luke 3:8). If you do not want to be the builders of God's Kingdom and His righteousness on earth, God will call other peoples.

Before the death of a great Christian man, Woodrow Wilson, his Secretary of War, Newton Baker, who is still alive, visited him and told him that all hopes for the creation of the League of Nations in Geneva were lost. Great in spirit but broken in body, Wilson gathered his last strength, and raising his wise head, he exclaimed: "But they cannot stop God." We who believe in God and His eternal righteousness could exclaim the same thing to the atheists: You cannot stop God. But God does not want the death of the sinner, but He wants all men to be saved (cf. 1 Tim. 2:4). This is why His divine voice was heard over Palestine nineteen centuries ago and why the echo of His voice resounds to this day in our ears: *Repent, for the Kingdom of Heaven is at hand* (Mat. 4:17).

God's kingdom and its righteousness sooner or later will be realized on earth.[1] It is up to us if we are going to participate in its construction. Today, on the day of the Nativity of Christ the Lord, I pray to Him that Christ God be born and always reborn in the soul of my people, that over the skies of my motherland and my people the song will always ring out: *Glory to God in the highest, and on earth peace, goodwill among men* (Luke 2:14).

Let this song of peace also find its way into the hearts and souls of our people that are scattered all over the great America, people who are living through the difficult days of shortages and uncertainties of tomorrow. May the God of peace come into the disturbed soul of my beloved flock, and may today, on the day of the Nativity of the Lord, in the soul of my people also be born faith in a better, happier future. And above all, I wish to everyone that—we no longer live, but that Christ may live in us (cf. Gal. 2:20). May our good God grant that our people correctly understand this terrible material crisis and that, at a time when the material treasures are being lost, our people do not lose their greatest treasure—their soul. *For what profit is it to a man if he gains the whole world, and loses his own soul* (Mat. 16:26)?

No matter how harsh and merciless the trials of our lives may be, we always ought to derive a lesson out of them for ourselves and for the salvation of our souls. Once I watched peasants mercilessly whipping their cattle, so the cattle would exit the burning barn and so that they would save their precious flock from the jaws of a horrific fire. Likewise, the Lord sometimes whips us and beats us with hunger, sickness, and various trials, in order to save us from spiritual death, which is more terrible than any physical death. Our wise people correctly estimated the value of the body and soul, the value of the earthly and heavenly, and said: "The earthly kingdom is short-lived; the heavenly is forever and ever." When someone commits a transgression and sin, our people do not threaten him with the law and jail, but they say: "Where is your soul going to go?" Tsar Lazar

---

[1] 2 Pet. 3:12–13: *Seeing then that all these things shall be dissolved, what manner of persons ought ye to be in all holy conversations and godliness, looking for and hasting unto the coming day of God, wherein the heavens being on fire shall be dissolved, and the elements shall melt with fervent heat? Nevertheless we, according to His promise, look for new heavens and a new earth, wherein dwelleth righteousness.*—Ed.

was glorified and he will be glorified as long as our people live, just because he despised the earthly kingdom and chose the heavenly. He made a wise decision because God said: *Seek first the kingdom of God, and everything else will be added to you* (Luke 12:31). The holy Tsar Lazar lost the earthly kingdom with his people, but he saved his soul and joined the Heavenly Kingdom. Together with his people he sought first of all the Kingdom of God, and everything else came by itself. As the logical consequence there also came the liberated Serbia. Had Lazar renounced the Kingdom of God, there would have been no Serbia, there would have been today no sons and daughters of our motherland and of our Holy Church.

Peace to you from God incarnate, dear brethren, and may the blessing of the Lord be upon you, your children and your households, and from me, your humble bishop, my love, my prayer for all of you, and my warm fatherly greeting.

CHRIST IS BORN!

Yours in God, humble intercessor
Bishop Mardarije

21ˢᵗ Archpastoral Epistle
of Bishop Mardarije
on Pascha

Mardarije, by God's grace Bishop of the Serbian Orthodox Diocese in America and Canada, to his dear clergy and people of his God-given diocese, on the day of the bright Resurrection of Christ, from the depth of his soul exclaims:

Christ is Risen!

Our people say that man learns as long as he lives. There is no greater teacher than personal experience. It is the most convincing teacher in life. How can you believe the cries of a hungry man if you yourself have never been hungry? How can you understand the cries and sighs of the sick if you have never been sick yourself?

And here I, your bishop, send this epistle to you, my spiritual flock, scattered all over the great America, in my new and rich experience, gained in suffering, pain, and ceaseless sighing over the last two years, wanting to tell you everything that is in my heart, as if in confession, to tell you about that which has filled my being with a faith even stronger than the one which was planted in my heart from my childhood. Confessing before you, I want just one thing, and that is to strengthen you in your faith in God, Who was, is, and will be, regardless of whether people believe in Him or not. This is my confession.

On a sunny day about two years ago I was decorating the park around the monastery church in Libertyville with about ten workers. Suddenly out of my chest a stream of blood started flowing. For three days the doctors could not stop the bleeding. They took me to the hospital. Two doctors diagnosed that my days in this world were numbered. In order to verify that claim, my closest coworkers called two well-known specialists in tuberculosis, one of whom was an old professor of medicine at the University of Chicago. Those two specialists said to the priests who were gathered around me to say good-bye that that night, during the night, or at the latest the next day, in the morning, I should die. The priests believed it. Who wouldn't? They were hearing this from those who were experts in the field. And they had to believe it even more because I had already given instructions for my burial at the monastery, and because the temperature and heartbeat of my sick body were at levels from which, according to the science of medicine, a man cannot return back to life. I was in a death-bed delirium and I did not recognize the people around me. And then suddenly, around midnight, I quietly said to the priests who were standing around me: "One of you, go to the monastery, serve Liturgy, bring the Holy Gifts, and give me Communion."

During the night, from time to time, I regained consciousness. In those moments my lips whispered a warm prayer to the Lord Christ. This was not an ordinary prayer. This was rather a direct conversation of a son with his Father. I felt the graceful presence of Christ and I prayed like this:

> Lord Christ and my God, I don't care if I die. I am not sorry to leave this world. I am ready to close my tired eyes and stand before Your righteous judgement seat, trusting that Your fatherly love and mercy will forgive me, if in my earthly life I did not act according to Your commandments, if I was not zealous enough in the great and responsible episcopal mission, which You through Your Church entrusted me with. You will forgive me, I know, because Your fatherly love is beyond measure. You will also forgive me because, from my childhood, from the sixteenth year of my life, I dedicated my life to serving You, Your altar, and Your people. I am not afraid of death. Personally, I am even looking forward to it, because in Your eternal Kingdom things will be incomparably easier for me than they have been in this sinful world. For me the transition from this life is not a transition into an unknown, desolate space with no substance or sense, but a transition into Your eternal Kingdom, which You promised to

all those who believe in You. But I beg of You, Heavenly Father and Lord Christ, pour out upon me, Your faithful servant, Your rich mercy, and leave me in this world a few more years, so that I can complete my service to my people and Church, in which You have mercifully elevated me to the greatest apostolic dignity. I would like to preach Your Holy Gospel with even more fervor, to even more warmly relate to my people that salvation is possible only through You and in You. Leave me on earth a little more that I may decorate the monastery of Your great saint Sava a little better. Extend the days and years of my life, if nothing else, then that I can help my old parent and his numerous family, whom a handful of people of no conscience, irresponsible people from the street, cloaked with a cover of modern morals, try to bring down to the level of a pauper, destroying the community of his home. I pray to You, O Lord my God, fulfill my prayer. Hear me in my weakness, in this night and this hour of death. You can do anything. You brought back the dead from the grave to life with one word. With the touch of Your fingers You gave eyesight back to the blind. I pray to You, this night, when I expect my departure from this world, touch my weak body with Your miraculous right hand and return life to me, which is now on its way to being extinguished. O Lord, let me get up from my death bed, and return to my dear people, and preach to them how You worked a miracle in me and gave me back my life. But not my will be done, but Your will be done, O Lord.

With those words I concluded my warmest prayer, bathed in warm tears, which freely fell on my pillow and I closed my tired eyes. I fell asleep and I saw a strange vision. People call it a dream. I saw myself walking, broken from the illness, hunched over, through the monastery gate toward my prepared tomb. Suddenly, above the monastery church, I saw a perfect bright circle descending toward the earth. An invisible force pulled me closer and closer to the bright circle. When I approached and came very close, I recognized in that bright circle the Holy Communion of Christ and out of that circle I heard the words: "Look at the multitudes of people on both sides of the monastery river. They are waiting for you. Go to them."

Soon it dawned. They woke me up. Through the open doors of my room, a fully vested priest with a chalice in his hand entered. There could have been no Confession, because I could not speak.

With tears of joy that I was receiving the Body and Blood of Christ for the last time, and with firm faith in eternal life beyond the grave, with faith which had never before been so illumined by the graceful presence of the kindest and most merciful, all-forgiving, heavenly Father and our Lord Jesus Christ, I partook of His Holy and most pure Body and Blood.

And what happened at that very moment, my dear brethren? That very moment my eyes opened wide. My reason, which had been darkened by the proximity of death, was suddenly illumined. The doctor who came to the hospital that morning, convinced that he would find me dead, entered through the door, allowed the priest who communed me to exit, nervously approached my bed, took my hand, measured my pulse, and suddenly, his face was radiant with joy. He repeated a couple of times that my heart was in excellent condition and that my pulse was normal. When he was convinced that my temperature was also normal, while it had been announcing my death the night before, this doctor, a Jew, exclaimed: "The bishop will live! This is a true miracle from God!"

Since then two years have passed, my dear brethren, and I, by God's grace, have advanced in my health, so that today the doctors and all the people who have known me over the past eighteen years here in America tell me that I have never in my life looked better than right now.

My conscience keeps telling me: "Why are you quiet? Why don't you tell the people about the miracle that God worked in you?" For two years I hesitated and hid the mystery of my healing, but I will not keep silent anymore. I will feel better when I relate this mystery to my people. And this is what I am doing. The faithful will believe this and they will be established in their faith even more, while the unbelievers will doubt. I am doing my duty toward God and His miraculous power ...

The content of my Paschal epistle for this year is unusual, my dearly beloved ones, but so is the event which I am relating to you. May God grant that many derive a spiritual benefit from this confession of mine. It testifies that God to this day works miracles and fulfills the prayers of those who believe in Him.

Therefore, my dear brethren, pray to God all the days of your lives, and God will give you help in need as He has delivered me. And as for me, I will dedicate my extended lifetime on earth even more, from now on, to the service to God and my dear people, declaring even more convincingly that our salvation is in the Lord. And if we die, we will resurrect in Him.

In the name of the resurrected Lord Christ, I exclaim to all of you the joyful and victorious greeting:

Christ is Risen!

Your warm intercessor in the Lord,
Bishop of America and Canada,
Mardarije

The Condition of Society

by Archimandrite Sebastian Dabović

How long will it thus go on! When will the baptized become active Christians, so that the pastors may give their attention to the conversion of the heathen? What a terrible battle we must fight. Already the fire of hell is in the world. Great cities are multiplying throughout the land. The farmer, as the word is defined in our dictionaries, is a thing of the past. It is now the land-owner with a mansion in the city, a yacht on the sea, and with a private train across the continent. There are comparatively but a few laborers in the fields—too poor to support families. The quiet country homes are becoming few, shall I say precious? I fear not so, because people are fast losing their ability to rightly estimate the value of things. Most of the cities in all the world are overcrowded. The female portion of the population is most conspicuous. A stupid craze after unwholesome fashions is the one all-absorbing passion of the majority of women. There is no room for gardens and yards; most of the children in San Francisco are actually brought up in the streets. Oh, how few of them feel the blessed influence of a Christian home! Young men and young women are continually "on the go," as they say. And this "go" is a nervous, unsteady rush to "keep up with the times." And after all their hurry nothing is left but steam and vapor, for they are empty, as empty as the changing and vanishing world can be. Yet they fret and inquire: "Where shall we go to and what shall we see? What shall we do? Oh! what can we do?" If you promenade along the broad avenue or pass through the narrow lane, if you visit the meeting halls in the city or look into the factories, everywhere you see that same all-devouring gaze of the bold young woman, who stares with a kind of artificial movement of the eyes. And sometimes you hear even so-called Christians say that it is a weakness of character in one who has the downcast eyes of modesty, the blush of innocence. Such people do not know the live sense and fine impulse of a pure conscience. When a young man puffs tobacco smoke or shows his teeth with a disapproving smile in the presence of and at the conversation of older people, then society is wrong; something is the matter with his family.

In view of all this, beloved, the preacher of the Word of God is obliged by a terrible oath he has given before he received the gift in Apostolic succession at his ordination, to present to you the whole of the Truth, not a part of it.

The number of unmarried people is increasing. And there are some married people who say: "We do not want children, because we want to have as much pleasure as possible." This is a false position, for in a Christian marriage one kind of pleasure is not allowed continually. Christians marry for the sake of God and His law as much as they do for themselves. But Christians who remain single renounce marriage and live holy for the sake of God and Him alone. Thus we find that the family tie is abused, as well as the single state. Courtship of young people just out of school is not to be advised, because it often leads to debauchery. A courtship running through long years also gives occasion to sin and a species of wrongdoing to God, for the heart and its love are stolen from God and thrown away on a man.

Throughout all the long centuries of Christianity there have been in the Church heroic members, young people of both sexes, who by the grace of God have kept their souls pure and intact, and have dedicated to the honor of God the noblest attribute of their human life, namely, an untarnished purity of soul and body. Such persons have had the courage and such unbounded confidence in God's assistance that, although living in the world and its dangers, though threatened by the cravings of their own individual passions and by the temptations of the devil, yet they have succeeded bravely in preserving this treasure even in a frail earthen vessel, have carried it uninjured through life's long journey here below, and have finally presented it to their Lord.

Christian heroes and heroines, you who have imitated or who still do imitate the sublime example of the Most Blessed Virgin, the

Church admires your spirit of sacrifice as she does that of the holy martyrs, who in a few hours finished their contest and proved their fidelity to God and their faith; because you have to combat, to suffer, and to sacrifice your whole life through. With joy and veneration do the angels look down upon you, for you resemble themselves. With motherly affection and with mighty power does the Holy Virgin Mary when you earnestly pray throw her sheltering omophorion around you, for you are her pupils and imitators. With the sweetness of divine love the heavenly Bridegroom will fill your heart and more than compensate you for the fleeting, transient, worldly love that you have laid down at His feet. The eternal Judge will find you waiting like the wise and prudent virgins who all through life carry in their hands the pure oblation of love and the burning light of good example. Therefore, faithful to the end, He will invite you to the eternal wedding feast in heaven. Amen.

From Sebastian Dabovich,
*Preaching in the Russian Church
or Lectures and Sermons by a Priest
of the Holy Orthodox Church*
(San Francisco: Cubery and Company, 1899),
pp. 160–64.

Thoughts on Fasting and Temperance

by Archimandrite Sebastian Dabović

MAN, having received his present being, consisting of a visible body and an intellectual, immaterial soul, is a being complex. But the nature and worth of both the just-named parts are not of equal value. The body is made as an instrument that is moved by the order of a ruler; the soul is designed to govern and command it, as the superior of an inferior. The soul, receiving from the intellect and reason the means by which it makes distinctions, may, possessing such a quality of distinction, separate the truly beautiful from its common imitation; it may perceive God as the Creator and Designer, not only of that which is underneath our feet and received by our senses, but that, also, which is hidden from the eyes, and which the immaterial mind may contemplate, having the power of imagination at its command.

Practicing, as the godly one, in righteousness and virtue, it aspires unto divine wisdom, and, obeying its laws and commands, withdraws as much as possible from the desires of the flesh, comes nearer to God, and strives by all its strength to ally itself with the good. The particular and most important object of this sacred philosophy is temperance; as it is the mind, which is not disturbed, but free of all influences of pollution, arising from the stomach or other senses, that has a continual action and contemplates the heavenly, the things pertaining to its own sphere.

And so it behooves us, the lovers of all things pure, the lovers of the word of God, yea—even Christians, to love the present time, which our holy Church has set apart for a special opportunity of obtaining greater grace in the sight of God. We should hail with joy such an opportunity! The time I refer to is Great Lent. We should love this fast as the teacher of sobriety, the mother of virtue, the educator of the children of God, the guardian of the unruly, the quiet of the soul, the staff of life, the peace that is firm and serene. Its importance and strictness pacifies the passions, puts out the fire of anger and wrath, cools and quiets the agitation produced by overeating. And, as in summer time, when the sweltering heat of the sun hangs over the ground, the northern breeze proves a blessing to the sufferers, scattering the closeness by its pleasant coolness, so does likewise fasting, destroying the overabundance of heat in the body, which is caused by gluttony. Proving to be of so much benefit to the soul, Lent brings the body no less benefit. It refines the coarseness of matter, releases the body of part of its burden, lightens the blood vessels that are often ready to burst with an overflow of blood, and prevents them from becoming clogged, which may happen as easily as it occurs with a water pipe, that, when being forced to maintain the abundance of water pressed into it by a powerful machine, bursts from the pressure. And the head feels light and clear when the blood vessels do not nervously beat, and the brain does not become clouded by the spreading of evaporations. Abstinence gives the stomach ease, which relieves it from a forced condition of slavery, and from boiling like a boiler, working with a sickly effort to cook the food it contains. The eyes look clear and undimmed, without the haze that generally shadows the vision of a glutton. The activity of the limbs is stable, that of the hand firm; the breath is regular and even, and not burdened by pent-up organs. The speech of him who fasts is plain and distinct; the mind is pure, and then it is that the mind shows forth its true image of God, when, as if in an immaterial body, it quietly and undisturbedly exercises the functions belonging to it. The sleep is quiet and free from all apparitions. Not to extend unnecessarily, we may sum up by saying that fasting is the common peace of the soul and body. Such are the beneficent results of a temperate life; and such are the precepts of a Christian life. It is a law of the Holy Church, which prescribes that we should fast during the Lenten season.

Do you not know that angels are the constant watchers and guardians of those that fast, just as the demons, those very friends of greasy stuffs, those lovers of blood and companions of drunkards, are the associates of those that give themselves up to debauchery and orgies during such a holy time as Lent? The angels and saints, as also the evil spirits, ally themselves with those they love; they become related with that which is pleasing to them. Every day in our life God points out a lesson to us concerning the eternal life, but we very seldom heed it; in a word, we generally don't care! Oh, is this not terrible to think of? And yet no one man will deliberately, so to speak, attempt to slight the Almighty Creator, no one who is capable of using his understanding in the very least degree. But yet, beloved brethren, we do it! We, day after day, in our worldly habits unconsciously say: "I don't care!" Have we a right to do anything at all unconsciously, when He, in Whose hand the very breath of our life flutters as a very weak, little thing, when He, I say, bestowed upon us this conscience? Over and over again we dare to directly disobey God's commands. It is a terrible thing to fall into the hands of the Living God (Heb. 10:31). But the Lord of Hosts is long-suffering, and to repentant Christians He is the Father of Mercies. Yet it behooves us, Christians, to zealously watch every step we take, to be sure that we are walking in the path that our Holy Church not only pointed out, but, as it were, even cut out for us by the stream of martyrs' blood, by the wisdom of the Holy Spirit abiding in the sainted bishops of the universal Councils, the night labor of praying and fasting fathers, and a host of pure, self-sacrificing, obedient women, such as Mary, Thecla, Barbara, Macrina. The Church says that in the time of Lent we must fast, and we should not disobey, because our Holy Church is the Church of God, and she tells us what God Himself wills that we should do. If we have all the learning of the nineteenth century, it will appear as a blank before the simple words of the Church, spoken in the power of the Spirit of God. We cannot, and we have no right (for who gave us such a privilege?), to excuse ourselves. We are with good intention, in simplicity of heart, to obey the commandments of the Church, and not worry about adapting ourselves to the ways of the Church, for when we obey with our whole heart, with a strong desire to fulfill the holy commandments, then our Holy Mother Church adapts herself to the weakness of her faithful children.

But let us turn back to the lesson pointed out for us. We may every day learn a new lesson about the next life, which is of so much importance, that the examples in this life are inexhaustible. Look around and observe. In this instance look into the kingdom of animals and birds. See the clean dove hovering over places that are clean, over the grain field, gathering seed for its young. Now look at the unsatiated raven, flapping its heavy wings around the meat market. And so we must strive to love a temperate life, that we may be beloved by angels, and hate all unnecessary luxury, so as not to fall with it into communion with demons.

Let us return with our memory to the commencement of our race, and experience will testify to that which we sometimes make light of. The law of fasting would not be given to us, had not the law of the first abstinence been transgressed. The stomach would not be named as an evil-minded thing, had not the pretext for pleasure entailed after it such consequences of sin. There would be no need of the plow and the laboring oxen, the planting of seed, the watering shower, the mutual change of the seasons of the year, the winter binding in fetters and the summer opening up all things. In a word there would be no need of such periodically repeating toil, had not we, through the mistaken pleasure of our first parents, condemned ourselves to this round of labor. Yet we were on the way of leading another kind of life, in comparison with what we see now, and which we hope to regain once more, when we are liberated from this life of passion by the resurrection. Such is the mercy of God's condescension towards us, that we should be again restored to the former dignity, which we had enjoyed through His love to man, and which mercy we did not carefully keep. Fasting is a type of the future life, an imitation of the incorruptible existence. There are no feastings and sensual gratifications over there.

Do not flee from the difficulty of fasting, but set up hope against the trial, and you will obtain the desired abstinence from food. Repeat to yourself the words of the pious: "Fasting is bitter, but paradise is sweet; thirst is tormenting, but the spring, from which he who drinks will thirst never again, is at hand." The body is importunate, but the immaterial soul is much stronger—strength is dead, but nigh is the resurrection. Let us say to our much-craving stomach what the Lord said to the tempter: Man shall not live by bread alone, but by every word of God (Luke 4:4). Fasting is not hunger, but a little abstinence from food, not an inevitable punishment, but a voluntary continence, not a servile necessity, but a free selection of the wise. Pray and you will be strengthened; call, and a prompt helper will come to your assistance.

From Sebastian Dabovich, *Preaching in the Russian Church, or, Lectures and Sermons by a Priest of the Holy Orthodox Church* (San Francisco: Cubery and Company, 1899), pp. 95–105.

Sincere Religion

by Archimandrite Sebastian Dabovich

W E LIVE in a peculiar age. No time has ever dawned upon the earth like the present era. Startling developments in the world of truth keep the minds of men, to some extent, constantly reaching out after it. More light! greater knowledge! is now the almost universal cry. Great discoveries in science have opened many new and hitherto unknown avenues to the greater physical development of the human family; and at the same time it may be said to be true, that the mental development of man has, to some extent, kept pace. In all this onward movement in the world of material and mental research, men turn to the representative of God among men, and inquire if in the religious world there are any developments; and we find that there are many and great changes in the religious world. Mark you—many and great changes in the world of religious opinion, but very little development in religious life!

Many a searching, although blind, mind has mistaken religion for some philosophical system. Too irreverent and profane handling of religion often makes of it a science, a pastime study. Now and again we come by the way of such who make religion a speculation; yes, and a speculation without a question as to its nature. Do you not know that religion is one of the qualities of your soul? An essential substance, I might say, to be plain, of your self-recognizing, self-satisfied, living spirit? Those who are convinced of this fact are not indifferent to religion. Indifferentism has no place in the serious life of one who seeks to be right-minded.

We hear it frequently remarked that it matters not what one believes if he does right. But if one does not believe right, he does not do the right thing—that is, if his belief is sincere and carried out in practice. If one believes that which is wrong, and still acts otherwise from force of circumstance, he is wrong in heart. A man may believe in polygamy, but the law and common custom may forbid its practice. He would be in outward life aright, but in heart would be a virtual polygamist. And if circumstances were favorable, his life would bear its legitimate fruit. And this is just as true of every other moral evil. It is all-important to believe right. Every false religion which has cursed mankind has started in a wrong belief. It might not have affected practical duties for a time, but the fruit finally developed. Thus, belief in that first lie of Satan's (Gen. 3:4) has borne its legitimate fruit in—first, the deification of the beautiful, and unnatural curiosity; second, self-love, delusion, and idol-worship; third, free-thinking, protesting, infidelity, and anarchy.

Beloved, when I gave all diligence to write unto you of the common salvation, it was needful for me to write unto you, and exhort you that ye should earnestly contend for the faith which was once delivered unto the saints (Jude 3). It is worthy, and more, too, it is a duty, to mention the fact that the large number of Bible-worshipers, who daily read the Holy Scriptures, will not see such passages as this. It is strange, yet it is plain to those who understand the human soul. What do those people think of such texts, and also of these: *I will build my church; and the gates of hell shall not prevail against it* (Matt. 16:18). *There is one body, and one Spirit, even as ye are called in one hope of your calling. One Lord, one faith, one baptism. One God and Father of all* (Eph. 4:4-6). *And there shall be one fold, and one Shepherd* (John 10:16). *Therefore, brethren, stand fast, and hold the traditions which ye have been taught, whether by word, or our epistle* (2 Thess. 2:15).

To read the Bible does not mean to be a Christian. One may go to church and also study the Holy Scriptures, and yet not be religious. One may be religious, and yet be laboring under false impressions, and also untruthful doctrine. If your friend requests you to do something for him, and you, knowing what he said, would still hesitate, had you not been positive of his own opinion of the request. If you are not always positive of a man's idea, even when you have his words, are you sure of God's opinion? Are you so elevated that you can read God's mind?

"Obey and believe in my doctrine," says Rome. "Be free and strive to create a belief for yourselves," say the Sects. But the Church calls to her own, "Let us love one another, that we may with one mind confess Father, Son, and Holy Spirit."

What is the Orthodox Church? This is the thought, which is repeated more than once in the closed closet of the heart; the question silently asked by the inquiring mind; and, beyond doubt, it is a proof of the quickening presence of the "Spirit of Truth, which abideth everywhere," stirring our souls to action superhuman, and to the contemplation of things which are above our comprehension.

Of late, the One Holy Catholic and Apostolic Church is often heard of, and the existence of an Orthodox Catholic Church has come before the notice of the reading masses in Western Europe and America. A grand revelation! And a heavenly blessing is reserved for all religious people who are striving in these latter times to be right-minded.

In the midst of Romanism and Protestantism, free from the fanaticism of a Pius,[2] or the indifferentism of a so-called liberalism, clear of modern congregationalism—almost daily crumbling into isms—we can see a glow, in the midst of this chaos, as if of a new spark created in a combustible mass, which is none other than the light once revealed to Adam, then faithfully preserved in the Church of the old dispensation, and finally entrusted to the *One* and only Church of God—the Alpha and Omega; this spark we now see illuminated to perfection by the new covenant of God with man, the pledge of which is no less than the ETERNAL WORD, the Only-begotten Son of God Himself—the man Jesus, who is the chief cornerstone of the Orthodox Catholic Church, which rests on the foundation of the Apostles, chosen and put into their places by the Supreme Architect—the Lord Jesus Christ. And behold, this is the Holy Orthodox and Universal (Catholic) Apostolic Church—still the ark of salvation for mankind. Could this stronghold, planned by God the Almighty, be obliterated, because of persecution and temptation, and because of the many that willfully stray away, which of themselves break into numerous sects, as the body deprived of life turns to dust? THE GATES OF HELL SHALL NOT PREVAIL AGAINST IT.

---

[2] Since this essay was published in 1898, this refers most likely to Pope Pius IX, who reigned from 1846 to 1878. He convened the First Vatican Council, which decreed the dogma of papal infallibility.—Ed.

We are all obnoxious to error and mistakes, and it is but natural that we should make due allowance for human weakness and ignorance. If God had left us in our higher concerns to our devices, we should be still groping in the dark like the heathen of old, whom God left to themselves, in order to show how utterly unable the natural man is to find and grasp the supernatural truth. God mercifully revealed to us His truth, and expects us to thankfully accept it, neither doubting nor denying it. Therefore, what in human concerns might be called a liberal concession to our opponents, would in religion be a foul treachery, opposite God's truth entrusted to His Church. It is not liberal, but indifferent, to regard all sorts of religion as equivalent; not to care to what religion one belongs, just as if one was as good or as bad as the other; or, to put it more forcibly, that the claim of one church to teach Christ's truths purely and completely, to the exclusion of all other churches, is not true, and is simply humbug. This is the principle of all worldly people, and it is a fashion to consider a conscientious religious church-life a downright nuisance, though one is still afraid to call it so. The crowd call it liberal not to make any distinction between the teaching of the different churches, just as if truth and untruth could exist one at the side of the other without any disrespect to God, the Author of truth. It is want of faith and conviction, or rather want of taking an interest in religion, that produces this baleful indifference.

It stands to reason that it is sinful to care so little for the revealed truth as to place it on a level with error. You will say, shall we then condemn our erring brethren? By no means. Christ forbids us to judge anybody, for only God knows whether our brother culpably holds the error, or whether he believes it to be the truth. But even if he believes his error to be the truth, error remains error, and never can become truth. Therefore, we must always condemn error, though we may not condemn the person erring, but must pity him that he takes error for truth. If you think it is all the same what a man believes, provided he is convinced that it is the truth, you are mistaken, for the heathen of old, the Jews, the Mohammedans, and the professors of all other religions, believe they possess the truth. Why, then, did God send His Only-begotten Son, Jesus Christ, into the world, if mankind could be saved without Him? Christ commanded His

Apostles and their successors to convert the world to Christianity, not to that sort of vague Christianity which we find in the numerous seditions which appropriate this name, but to His one Church, *which is the foundation and pillar of the truth* (1 Tim. 3:15), and against which the gates of hell can never prevail. He who believes in these words of Christ can never be indifferent to which Church he belongs, nor can he be indifferent whether his friends or acquaintances continue in error. Therefore, it is his first duty never to countenance religious indifference. Those who will study the doctrine of the Church, not in the errors and weakness of human superstitions and failings, but in her own divinely inspired rites and institutions, will appreciate the matchless purity of our beloved Church. Let us not be misunderstood. We do not assume to ourselves any prerogative of goodness; on the contrary, woe unto us who have so little profited by the perfect holiness of our Mother Church. The best among us fall grievously short of the ideal of the Church, which towers high above us, bearing aloft the standard of the Cross.

Truly glorious and divine is the plan of our Church, but beware of judging her by the failures and errors of her unworthy children.

In her daily Liturgy our Mother—the Church—calling the faithful to prayer, teaches us thus: *Let us pray to the Lord for the peace of the whole world, the good estate of the holy churches of God, and the union of them all.*

For the unity of the Faith, and the communion of the Holy Spirit making request, let us commend ourselves and one another and all our life to Christ the God.

From Rev. Sebastian Dabovich,
The Lives of Saints and
Several Lectures and Sermons
(San Francisco: The Murdoch Press, 1898),
pp. 174–83.

St. Sebastian of Jackson (1863–1940).
Commemorated November 17/30.

IV
Appendices

Father Sebastian Dabovich

by Saint Nikolai (Velimirović) of Žiča

First published in the *Serb National Federation
Commemorative Book,* 1951.

IN THE TIME of Lincoln's presidency there existed already a notable Serbian colony in San Francisco. Among other immigrants
there were two brothers, Nikola and Ilija Dabovich. They came from
the village Sassovici in the district of Herzeg Novi, Bocca of Cattaro.
They were related to other two well-known Serbian families, Shim-
rak and Radojevich, both from the same district in Bocca.

Ilija Dabovich had a pretty large family of lovely girls and two
fine boys, Stefan and Jovan. And this Jovan, born on June 9, 1863,
was the late Archimandrite Sebastian Dabovich, the first American-
born Serbian priest, the first Serbian Orthodox Missionary, and the
first head of the Serbian Orthodox Mission in America.

The first time I heard of Father Sebastian was in the house of
Cheddo Mijatovich, the former ambassador of the Kingdom of Serbia at the court of St. James in London, about forty years ago. Mijatovich showed me two books written in English by the Rev. Sebastian Dabovich and published in the United States. He praised the
books as being very informative about the Orthodox Church and
faith, and he praised very highly the author of those books whom
he knew well. Said Mijatovich: "My friend Father Dabovich never
fails to see me whenever he arrives in London. He is a real church-
man, knowing his business well and caring for nothing else."

During the First World War in 1915 I arrived in San Francisco.
Father Dabovich met me at the station. He introduced me to many
Serbs in that city. He took me to the Russian church, of which the

rector then was Father Theodore, who married one of his sisters. This Father Theodore later on became the famous Metropolitan of the Russian Church in America, and died in 1950.

Father Dabovich was closely connected with the Russians. As a young layman he went to Russia to study Theology. In Russia he became a monk, changing his name from Jovan to Sebastian. By the Russian Archbishop he was appointed the head (*Nachelnik*) of the Serbian Church Mission in America. The Russian Archbishop, later the great Patriarch Tikhon, made him Archimandrite and gave him a golden cross. And yet his relations with the Russians had not been always smooth and friendly. Conflicts arose several times, as for instance in Jackson and Alaska. In Jackson, California, there was a large Serbian colony, but with out a church. In 1894 Father Dabovich urged the Serbs to build a church. They were numerous and well-paid, working in a gold mine. They all agreed and started collecting money. Father Dabovich asked and received a contribution from the "Canada" Company which owned the mine. And so the church, dedicated to St. Sava, appeared on a dominating hill in Jackson, in the center of the Serbian cemetery. The Russian Bishop demanded that that church should be chartered as a Russian church. Father Dabovich, supported by the Jackson Serbs, vehemently opposed. And before the case was brought to the law court Father Dabovich succeeded in procuring a Serbian charter for the church. And this was the first Serbian church built on the soil of the New World.

Then in Alaska. There again Father Dabovich succeeded in constructing a small Serbian church of St. Sava in spite of Russian opposition. He converted to Christianity several Eskimo villages. The Russians claimed them for themselves. Similar conflicts happened in Galveston and Cincinnati. He was a righteous man, and as such, and as an American, he could not bear the too much grasping by anybody, and not even by the Russians, under whose ecclesiastic authorities he worked. But he was not a man of lasting grudge and enmity. Generally speaking he was a friend and admirer of the Russian Church. And the Russians respected him.

He went on from place to place preaching the Gospel and rousing the Serbs to build their own churches. The people responded to his call, and they built churches in several places, as in Los Angeles and Chicago. Of his activity in Chicago, the poet Proka Jovkich wrote enthusiastically 1905 in the Serbian paper *Srpska Nezavisnost,* edited by Veljko Radojevich in San Francisco. In Chicago Dabovich organized a parish and erected a chapel on the same spot where now stands the magnificent Serbian church of the Resurrection. He was the first parish priest in that church. Proka Jovkich, helping Father Sebastian and seeing his evangelic zeal, decided to become a monk himself. But later he abandoned the idea. While in Chicago Dabovich started the first Serbian Church paper, *Herald of the Serbian Church Mission.* But he could not stay for long in one place. In 1917 Rev. Petar Stiyachich replaced him in that great city, and he went on with his apostolic mission all over America from coast to coast. Thus many times he visited the lonely Serbian families in deserts and wildernesses to administer Holy Sacraments and bring consolation. He crossed the Atlantic 15 times and the Pacific 9 times. In Tokyo the Russian Archbishop Nikolai offered him to stay and serve in the Russian Mission in Japan. But he was by vocation a wandering missionary, and could not stay there for long. But God sent another Serbian clergyman after him to Japan who stayed longer in the Russian Mission. That was Rev. Georgy Kodzich, a very remarkable man by his high learning and strict asceticism. This man, as an Archmandrite in San Francisco having no parish, worked as a manual laborer and acquired a modest house of his own, in which he arranged a chapel of St. John the Baptist and by his last will bequeathed it to the Serbian people in that westernmost great city. Thus what Father Dabovich had not done in his native city Father Kodzich did. Both of these men of God were candidates for Serbo-American bishops after the First World War. But it was fated otherwise. The true servants of the Lord are measured by their heart and character and not by a high hierarchical rank.

Archimandrite Dabovich could have been a bishop even in 1907. The Russian Archbishop wanted to ordain him as a Russian bishop for the Serbian people. But the Serbs did not want it that way. Archbishop Tikhon was sorry about that. He was eager to show his appreciation of Father Dabovich for all his wonderful work. Failing to make him a bishop, he did something else. Once when he celebrat-

ed the Holy Liturgy in the Serbian church in Chicago, he presented
our Archimandrite with a precious mitre, which was worth 1,000
roubles in gold. But Father Dabovich quickly sold that precious gift
and gave it to the church towards paying its debts. Such a man was
he. He was absolutely unselfish. He remembered well the words of
the apostle: "The love of money is the root of all evil" (1 Tim. 6:10).
His poverty amazed me when I met him once in New York in 1921.
I invited him to lunch. Blushing, he said, "Thank you; I just bought
a roll of bread with my last five cents." And salary? None. He lived
on people's freely given donations. And still, even with empty pockets, he planned new journeys to Alaska, to Japan, and of course to
Europe.

"But you are without means!" I remarked.

He smiled with his usual childlike and fascinating smile and
quoted the Bible: *"The Lord will provide"* (cf. Gen. 22:8). And marvelously enough, the Lord always provided for His faithful servant.

He was a sincere and convinced believer and a Christian missionary of world-scope. He traveled restlessly and preached and lec-
tured indefatigably. He composed books, wrote articles, epistles,
and thousands of private letters to laymen and priests with needed
explanations, exhortations and encouragements. He spoke and
wrote in Serbian, English, and Russian. His clumsy handbag was
always full with New Testaments, religious booklets, printed sermons and tracts. Also with small crosses for boys and girls. All this
he distributed freely. He never visited a Serbian family empty-hand-
ed. He remembered the apostolic words: *It is more blessed to give
than to receive* (Acts 20:35).

Father Dabovich was well known among the Serbs in America
and Canada. But not only among the Serbs, but among the Russians
and other Orthodox peoples as well. He made many friends among
the leaders of other denominations. Often I was asked by the Episcopalians and others: "Do you know Father Dabovich?" He was
decorated by the King of Serbia, by the Tsar of Russia, by the Prince
of Montenegro, and by the Patriarch of Jerusalem.

When he crossed the Atlantic for the 15th time and came to
Serbia, he remained there until his end. Patriarch Varnava gave him
an apartment in the Patriarchate, where he stayed until 1938. Then

he moved to Žiča, where he stayed with us for some time, then again to Herceg Novi. On his way to and fro he was steadily accompanied by Rev. Jovan Rapaich, whom he loved most of all and who took true filial care of the old man. Finally he returned definitely to Žiča, his last resort. He stayed with us until the end of 1940. From there he wrote many letters to his American friends. In a letter to Mr. Niko Mussich he wrote: "My body is getting weaker and weaker. I would like to see once more the Golden Gate. All my dearest memories from childhood are concentrated in San Francisco and in the country in which I was born." This letter has been published in I. Palandech's *Ujedinjeno Srpstvo,* March 6, 1941.

I visited him frequently, asking how the brothers served him. His heart was failing. Father Rapaich was with him day and night. The last time, on my return from the diocese, I went to see him. Sitting in an armchair he was breathing heavily and spoke in a whisper.

"Do you have any wish, Father?" I asked.

"Only the Kingdom of Heaven."

He spoke no more. These were his last words, representative of his entire career on earth. After that he gave up his spirit. He died on November 30, 1940.

The next day he was buried in the monastery's cemetery alongside another famous archimandrite, Father Raphael, formerly the Superior of the great Serbian monastery Hilandar on the Holy Mountain, who died in Žiča in 1937. During the night the season's first snow had covered the earth, and it was cold. Yet His Excellency the American Ambassador Arthur Bliss Lane sent the American Consul General from Belgrade to represent him at the burial. For Father Sebastian was an American citizen. Besides, Mr. Bliss Lane had great personal devotion to him, calling him "my spiritual father Dabovich."

So ended the earthly pilgrimage of a great servant of Christ and the greatest Serbian missionary of modern times. He was a missionary by words, by deeds, and—what is the greatest of all—by his personal character. He was a viceless man. Meek and unpretentious, he was positive and constructive in all his words and works. He never engaged in fruitless polemics. Externally he was a little, lean man, with a beard. Just the kind of priest the Serbian immigrants liked, remembering their bearded priests in the Old Country. And behold, he was American-born and not an immigrant. But his conviction was that an Orthodox priest ought to be recognizable as Orthodox by his exterior, too.

This of course is not a full biography but only a short survey or digest of the life of a man of God who for 53 years in the priesthood worked as a diligent bee to the glory of Christ our Saviour. Yea, and who worthily and nobly represented three great values: Orthodoxy, America and Serbia, equally loving all the three and equally serving all three.

Ten years have already passed since his death. Here is a man who indebted all the Serbian race, especially all the Serbs and all the Serbian organizations in America. Should that man remain without a monument or any sign of honor on American soil? He does not need it. He did not wish it. All he wished to his last breath was the Kingdom of Heaven, which I believe he has obtained by the grace of his Lord. But his people need it; his posterity needs it. The Serbian people always cultivated the noble virtue of gratitude. Let them express their traditional gratitude to this remarkable Serbian—Father Sebastian Dabovich.

To:
The Holy Hierarchical Synod of
the Serbian Orthodox Church

For:
The Holy Hierarchical Assembly of
the Serbian Orthodox Church
at its May Session in 2014
Libertyville, Illinois, USA

December 6, 2013

PETITION

TO THE HOLY HIERARCHICAL ASSEMBLY OF THE SERBIAN ORTHODOX CHURCH

Subject:
Recommendation for entering into
the Diptychs (Calendar) of the Saints of
Bishop Mardarije of Libertyville and
Archimandrite Sebastian of Jackson

Your Holiness and dear Brother Hierarchs in Christ,

The Almighty Lord glorified in Trinity, Who Himself only is Holy (Lev. 11:44-45; 2 Pet. 1:16), according to His miraculous providence is "incarnate" by the Holy Spirit in time and space as "wondrous in His Saints" (Ps. 67:36), granting through those pleasing to Him the blessings of incorruptibility to God's People and the whole universe. The Church "commemorates" these saints pleasing to God through liturgical glorification and the entering into the calendar of the saints. According to the ancient tradition of the One and Only, Holy, Catholic and Apostolic Church of Christ, Christians are called to carry on the work of the apostolic teaching and mission of the salvific Word of God, Christ the God-man, and to glorify all those who did this work in their time.

Two such newly proclaimed teachers equal to the apostles, who blossomed like beautiful flower stems on the Pan-Orthodox field of the North American continent, are the servants of God: Hierarch Mardarije (Uskoković), Bishop of the first Serbian diocese in North America, and Archimandrite Sebastian (Dabović), the first Orthodox priest born in America. Work on this field was done by several already glorified saints: Juvenaly (+1796) and Herman of Alaska (+1836), Peter of California (+ca. 1815), Innocent of Moscow (+1879), Alexis Toth (+1909), Raphael of Brooklyn (+1915), Tikhon the Confessor (+1925), Nikolai of Žiča (+1956), Varnava of Hvostno (+1964), John of San Francisco (+1966), and others. The Lord wanted the sons of the Serbian people to be among the first in this work and to deliver the first American Orthodox priest.

✼

Mardarije Uskoković (1889–1935) was the Bishop of the Diocese of America and Canada from 1926 until his repose on December 12, 1935. Born in Montenegro, tonsured in Studenica Monastery, Serbia, educated in Moscow, Saint Petersburg and elsewhere in the Russian Empire, called and placed to work in the Church and with the people in the diaspora in North America, Mardarije was manifested as a man of an entirely unusual spiritual format. His truly missionary work extended from the very end of Eastern Europe in distant Russia to the very western end of even more distant America. In that sense his spiritual radiance, but also glorification as a saint, is a blessing to all the Churches, and serves as an inexhaustible spring of inspiration for the Christians of the New World, Serbia, Russia, and beyond.

This God-pleasing man of a saintly image founded the Church life of our people in North America and, aside from that, he built the monastery of Saint Sava in the time of Great Depression, in the end of 1920s and the beginning of 1930s of the 20th century. During his life Mardarije went through great deprivations, and somebody coined the phrase: "He is building the church while starving to death." At the time when the monastery was built, it was the center of the newly founded Diocese of America and Canada. The land on which the monastery was built was bought by Bishop Mardarije himself. His body was buried on December 18, 1935, in the monastery church. In his testament he wrote:

"This holy monastery, as a place of assembly for Serbs in America, and the common house of prayer, as an eternal house of God, I leave as a heritage to my dear Serbian people so that they can after my death keep it and improve it, and so that they can leave it to their offspring in this New World as a beautiful monument of their national and religious conscience, and so that everyone to eternity can know and see, here on the other side of the Atlantic Ocean, that far from their motherland there were Serbs here. For all those Serbian men and women who helped me during the 18 years of work in America and thus eased my heavy burdens of governing the Serbian Church here, I pray to God to reward them with His mercy, and as for me, I leave to them and their homes my episcopal blessing."

✳

Six years ago, we celebrated the return of archimandrite **Sebastian Dabović** in Western America. The earthly remains of the first American Orthodox priest, apostle, and missionary, born in 1863 in San Francisco, reposed on November 30, and buried in Žiča in 1940, were transferred to Jackson, California, in 2007. Upon arrival, his body was buried inside the first Serbian Orthodox Church in America, which he founded in 1892, at the Serbian Orthodox cemetery in Jackson. On that occasion a great multitude of Orthodox believers gathered in Jackson, and they participated in the liturgical celebration led by six of our Orthodox hierarchs (from America, Serbia, Bulgaria, Australia, and Russia) and a great number of priests. In the Diocese of Western America an annual commemoration of Father Sebastian has been instituted already, and there are a number of clergy who already commemorate Sebastian as a saint in the liturgical dismissal, adding him thus to the holy enlighteners of the American land, like the Alaskan saints Tikhon, Herman, and Juvenaly, and then, Raphael of Brooklyn, Peter the Aleut, John of San Francisco (Maksimović), Nikolai of Žiča, Varnava the Confessor (Nastić), and others.

Archimandrite Sebastian is known all over America by his tireless and fruitful missionary and apostolic work, by his sermons in the English, Serbian, and Russian languages, and by a number of books that he wrote for the sake of the mission (both in English and

Serbian). Having built the first Serbian Orthodox Church in America, Father Sebastian built himself into the foundations of Orthodoxy in America. The newest hagiography (the writing of hieromonk Damascene of Platina, in English and Serbian) testifies to his exceptional struggle.

Father Sebastian also undertook missionary travels to the Orthodox mission in Japan, which for the longest time interested and inspired him. Saint Nikolai of Žiča noted that Father Sebastian had crossed the Atlantic Ocean fifteen times and the Pacific Ocean nine times during his life. When he performed the funeral service for Father Sebastian Dabović in Žiča Monastery in 1940, Saint Nikolai of Žiča addressed him, among other things, as a saint ("Saint Sebastian, the missionary of America").

The awareness of the apostolic and didactic sanctity of Sebastian Dabović and Mardarije Uskoković has been greatly developed already, especially in parish churches and monasteries, homes and cells of prayer and asceticism. The honoring of these two men, as those pleasing to God and as apostolic enlighteners, has been widespread among Orthodox Americans, who see Sebastian as "their own." A rising number of icons testify to this. The Orthodox Church in America (OCA) has already decided to "canonize" Sebastian Dabović, of which the Serbian Church was informed by the primate of that Church (the letter of the primate of OCA in 2008), expecting that the Serbian Patriarchate would do the "canonization" first.

In this decade we commemorate several important dates here on the North American continent; and before any others, the 95th anniversary of the founding of the first Serbian Diocese of America and Canada for the "new" continent is commemorated. This founding of our diocese elevated the life of our compatriots and our Church to a traditional episcopal and diocesan level. It is in the image of Bishop Mardarije Uskoković, the first Serbian bishop on this continent, that the deep common longing of our ancestors who immigrated to the New World was crowned in a most beautiful way. They courageously decided to set out for a foreign land, not hesitating because of the inevitable difficulties that would come, but going forward inspired by their deep faith, their Orthodox Church identity, and their honorable ancestral heritage. They felt and knew that loyalty to the Church and the unwavering fight for the building of the community and for the integration of oneself into the organism of the community are far more important than personal interests and ambitions.

With care for the awareness of the importance of unity, which they inherited from their old country, our ancestors assembled here, in the beginning oftentimes forming parishes together with our Russian and Greek Orthodox brothers, always remaining open and ready to witness evangelical love for their new non-Orthodox neighbors. Difficult circumstances in the church life in America prompted our ecclesiastical pioneers to unite and strengthen our Church communities by electing a first bishop for Canada and America. This first stage of the thorny path toward ecclesiastical unity, in which Saints Nikolai Velimirović, Mardarije Uskoković, and Sebastian Dabović were greatly involved, has produced its fruit precisely in recent times, as it allowed for a complete overcoming of the administrative disagreements of our dioceses.

Among many other laborers in this blessed field, all of whom are known to God, we should point out the merits of the recently reposed in the Lord Metropolitan Christopher. For the sake of further strengthening and establishing our Church life and witness in America, it is necessary to declare the unity of all Orthodox people through keeping communion with each other; and for this purpose the bishops of all Orthodox peoples in America have been working together in a common episcopal assembly for North America.

At the time when in North America we celebrate ninety years of the first diocese in America and Canada, and while we are completing the administrative unity of the entire Serbian jurisdiction, adding to the calendar of the saints of these two Serbs, Bishop Mardarije (Uskoković) of Libertyville and Archimandrite Sebastian (Dabović), the first Orthodox priest born in America, is a recognition of their glorification by the Lord and the people. It is also a fulfillment of a debt toward the heritage of these enlighteners equal to the apostles.

Therefore, we, Orthodox bishops, with the whole fullness of the Church in North and South America, assembled in our session of the Episcopal Council on December 5 and 6, 2013, consider that time has come that **we petition the Holy Hierarchal Assembly of our Local Church to add the names of Archimandrite Sebastian and Bishop Mardarije, the clergymen and the preachers of the Gospel, men pleasing to God with their holy lives, the inspirers of many missionaries—into the Diptychs of the Saints, into the Eortologion or the Calendar of the Saints of the Orthodox Church, and then that this holy act of the Assembly be made known to the other Orthodox Churches around the world.**

May these jubilees that we celebrate in America remind all of us of the efforts of our ancestors and direct us to the sacred goal of unity in Christ and His Holy Orthodox Church.

We ask the Holy Assembly that the day of the annual celebration of Bishop Mardarije be December 12, and of Father Sebastian—November 30, when Liturgy will be served, and their already written services will be sung (troparion, kontakion and other hymns) and their holy icons will be piously venerated.

Episcopal Council:
Metropolitan of Montenegro and the Coastlands Amfilohije
[Bishop-Administrator of Buenos Aires and South and Central America—trans.]
Bishop of Canada Georgije,
Bishop of New Gračanica and Midwestern America Longin,
Bishop of Eastern America Mitrofan,
Bishop of Western America Maksim

ИРИНЕЈ

БОЖЈОМ МИЛОШЋУ

ПРАВОСЛАВНИ АРХИЕПИСКОП ПЕЋКИ, МИТРОПОЛИТ БЕОГРАДСКО-КАРЛОВАЧКИ И ПАТРИЈАРХ СРПСКИ,
СА СВИМ ЧЛАНОВИМА СВЕТОГ АРХИЈЕРЕЈСКОГ САБОРА СРПСКЕ ПРАВОСЛАВНЕ ЦРКВЕ,
СВОЈ ДУХОВНОЈ ДЕЦИ СВОЈОЈ У ОТАЧАСТВУ И РАСЕЈАЊУ,
БЛАГОДАТ ВАМ И МИР ОД БОГА ОЦА НАШЕГА И ГОСПОДА ИСУСА ХРИСТА И ДУХА СВЕТОГА УТЕШИТЕЉА!

Изволи се Светоме Духу и нама (Дап. 15:28) у свештеном Сабору архијереја Православне Српске Цркве, на славу Оца и Сина и Духа Светога, Бога нашега, дивнога у Светима Својима, ради духовног добра и свеукупног напретка наше помесне Цркве и целе Једне, Свете, Саборне и Апостолске Цркве Христове, да прибројимо Сабору Светих блаженопочившег епископа МАРДАРИЈА који је Бога прославио својим животом и делима и кога је Господ већ прославио дивним знамењима и свенародним поштовањем.

Проглашавајући га светим христоносним Богоугодником Цркве Православне, молимо се Господу да његово сведочење Једног Човекољупца, и његов живи пример вере и љубави, послуже свима нама, као позив да му следујемо и прослављамо га у Цркви Христовој божанственим службама и похвалним песмама. Ово прослављање дарује Цркви Божјој велику духовну радост и благодарност Живоме Господу.

Молитвама светог оца нашег Мардарија, Пресвета Тројице, Боже наш, помилуј и спаси нас.

Једноме Свемудроме Богу Оцу, кроз Исуса Христа Господа нашега, у Духу Светоме, слава и величанство, моћ и власт, сада и увек, и у векове векова. Амин.

ДАНО У ПАТРИЈАРШИЈИ СРПСКОЈ У БЕОГРАДУ
ДАНА 29/16. маја 2015. године - АСБрој 109/уап.260

Председник
Светог архијерејског сабора
ДЕМ и Патријарх српски

[потпис]

Чланови
Светог архијерејског сабора

архиепископ охридски   епископ крањски

Митрополит црногорско-приморски   † епископ шумадијски *[потпис]*

Митрополит загребачко-љубљански   епископ браничевски

It seemed good to the Holy Spirit and us (Acts 15:28) that at the priestly Assembly of Hierarchs of the Serbian Orthodox Church, to the glory of God, Father and Son and Holy Spirit, who is glorious in His Saints, and for the spiritual good and overall progress of our local Church and the entire One, Holy, Catholic and Apostolic Church of Christ, to add to the Synaxis of Saints Bishop MARDARIJE of blessed repose, who had glorified God with his life and works and whom the Lord has already glorified through precious signs and reverence of all people.

Proclaiming him a holy, Christ-bearing God-pleaser of the Orthodox Church, we pray to the Lord that his witness of the Only Lover of man, and his living examples of faith and love be an invitation to us all that we follow and glorify him in Christ's Church in the divine services and through hymns of praise. This glorification bestows upon God's Church a great spiritual joy and thanksgiving to the Living Lord.

Through the prayers of our Holy Father Mardarije, O Most Holy Trinity, our God, have mercy upon us and save us.

To the Only All-Wise God the Father, through Jesus Christ our Lord, and the Holy Spirit, glory and majesty, power and dominion, now and ever, and unto the ages of ages. Amen.

Given at the Serbian Patriarchate in Belgrade
May, 29/16, 2015 – AS No. 109/recording 260

President of the Holy Assembly of Bishops
Archbishop of Pec, Metropolitan of Belgrade-Karlovci and
Serbian Patriarch IRINEJ
Members of the Holy Assembly of Bishops

епископ горњокарловачки

митрополит аустралијско-новозеландски

епископ шабачко-ваљевски

епископ крушевачки

епископ западноевропски   епископ славонски † *[потпис]*

епископ милешки   епископ аустријско-швајцарски

                                                      епископ франкфуртски и све Немачке

                                                      епископ тимочки *[потпис]*

ИРИНЕЈ
БОЖЈОМ МИЛОШЋУ
ПРАВОСЛАВНИ АРХИЕПИСКОП ПЕЋКИ, МИТРОПОЛИТ БЕОГРАДСКО-КАРЛОВАЧКИ И ПАТРИЈАРХ СРПСКИ,
СА СВИМ ЧЛАНОВИМА СВЕТОГ АРХИЈЕРЕЈСКОГ САБОРА СРПСКЕ ПРАВОСЛАВНЕ ЦРКВЕ,
СВОЈ ДУХОВНОЈ ДЕЦИ СВОЈОЈ У ОТАЧАСТВУ И РАСЕЈАЊУ,
БЛАГОДАТ ВАМ И МИР ОД БОГА ОЦА НАШЕГА И ГОСПОДА ИСУСА ХРИСТА И ДУХА СВЕТОГА УТЕШИТЕЉА!

ИЗВОЛИ СЕ СВЕТОМЕ ДУХУ И НАМА (Дап 15,28) У СВЕШТЕНОМ САБОРУ АРХИЈЕРЕЈА ПРАВОСЛАВНЕ СРПСКЕ ЦРКВЕ, НА СЛАВУ ОЦА И СИНА И ДУХА Светога, Бога нашега, дивнога у Светима Својима, ради духовног добра и свеукупног напретка наше помесне Цркве и целе једне, Свете, Саборне и Апостолске Цркве Христове, да прибројимо Сабору Светих преподобног архимандрита СЕВАСТИЈАНА који је Бога прославио својим животом и делима и кога је Господ већ прославио дивним знамењима и свенародним поштовањем.

Проглашавајући га преподобним христоносним богоугодником Цркве Православне, молимо се Господу да његово сведочење Јединог Човекољупца, и његов живи пример вере и љубави, послуже свима нама, као позив да му следујемо и прослављамо га у Цркви Христовој божанственим службама и похвалним песмама. Ово прослављање дарује Цркви Божјој велику духовну радост и благодарност Живоме Господу.

Молитвама преподобног оца нашег Севастијана, Пресвета Тројице, Боже наш, помилуј и спаси нас.

Јединоме Свемудроме Богу Оцу, кроз Исуса Христа Господа нашега, у Духу Светоме, слава и величанство, моћ и власт, сада и увек, и у векове векова. Амин.

ДАНО У ПАТРИЈАРШИЈИ СРПСКОЈ У БЕОГРАДУ
ДАНА 29/16. маја 2015. ГОДИНЕ - АСБрој 110/уап.261

Председник
Светог архијерејског сабора
АЕМ и Патријарх српски

(signature)

Чланови
Светог архијерејског сабора

Архиепископ охридски   Епископ ваљевски

Митрополит црногорско-приморски   *(signature) John*

Митрополит загребачко-љубљански   Епископ браничевски

It seemed good to the Holy Spirit and us (Acts 15:28) that at the priestly Assembly of Hierarchs of the Serbian Orthodox Church, to the glory of God, Father and Son and Holy Spirit, who is glorious in His Saints, and for the spiritual good and overall progress of our local Church and the entire One, Holy, Catholic and Apostolic Church of Christ, to add to the Synaxis of Saints the Venerable Archimandrite SEBASTIAN, who had glorified God with his life and works and whom the Lord has already glorified through precious signs and reverence of all people.

Proclaiming him a holy, Christ-bearing God-pleaser of the Orthodox Church, we pray to the Lord that his witness of the Only Lover of man, and his living examples of faith and love be an invitation to us all that we follow and glorify him in Christ's Church in the divine services and through hymns of praise. This glorification bestows upon God's Church a great spiritual joy and thanksgiving to the Living Lord.

Through the prayers of our Venerable Father Sebastian, O Most Holy Trinity, our God, have mercy upon us and save us.

To the Only All-Wise God the Father, through Jesus Christ our Lord, and the Holy Spirit, glory and majesty, power and dominion, now and ever, and unto the ages of ages. Amen.

Given at the Serbian Patriarchate in Belgrade
May, 29/16, 2015 – AS No. 110/recording 261

President of the Holy Assembly of Bishops
Archbishop of Pec, Metropolitan of Belgrade-Karlovci and
Serbian Patriarch IRINEJ
Members of the Holy Assembly of Bishops

Епископ крушевачки

Епископ славонски

Епископ аустријско-швајцарски

Епископ франкфуртски и све Немачке

Епископ тимочки

✳

The Glorification of
Saints Mardarije and Sebastian

THE HOLY Assembly of Hierarchs of the Serbian Orthodox Church during its regular session on May 29, 2015, added the names of Bishop Mardarije (Uskoković) of Libertyville, and Archimandrite Sebastian (Dabović) of San Francisco and Jackson, clergymen and preachers of the Gospel, God-pleasing servants of holy life, and inspirers of many missionaries, to the Dyptich of Saints (Calendar of Saints) of the Orthodox Church. Glory to God! Once again, through the lives of these two saints, we see our Orthodox Church as a faith that produces holy persons, "enriches the world with saints" and insists on an ethos of holiness.

This is a wonderful blessing for all of us Orthodox Christians in America, and for the whole Orthodox Church throughout the world. When one thinks of the tremendous sacrifices that these two holy apostles made, and the many sorrows that they endured, one is especially gratified that they are now universally recognized as being among the Church's luminaries. The feast of Holy Hierarch Mardarije will be celebrated on November 29/December 12, while that of the Venerable Sebastian will be celebrated on November 17/30.

The Western American Diocese of the Serbian Orthodox Church in North and South America plans to celebrate the public and liturgical glorification of the new saints at St. Steven's Cathedral in Alhambra, California, on September 5, 2015. The Serbian Patriarch, His Holiness Irinej, will lead the liturgical festivities, accompanied by the ruling hierarchs of the Orthodox Church in the USA. Many civil dignitaries and special invited guests will take part in the celebrations.

✳

Holiness: A Forgotten Vision?

by Metropolitan John of Pergamon

THE TERM "saint" or "sanctity" (holiness) is something entirely irrelevant and foreign to our time, and to the civilization and the quests of contemporary Man. Which parents nowadays have the ambition of making their children "saints"? Which of our schools and educational programs cultivate sanctity or present it as a vision and as a model? The "successful" person of our time, as well as the ideal of contemporary education and our civilization is not in the least the "good and benevolent" person of classical times. Instead, it is the one who can achieve wealth, comforts and social emergence—this is what parents want of their children, this is what our educational systems chiefly aspire to, this is what the mass media cultivate, and this is the dream of the majority of our young generation.

Indeed, in a society that regards **unemployment** as its most serious problem and is governed by the **anxiety** of how to increase its per capita income, for one to speak of saints and sanctity constitutes a challenge—or rather, a cause for laughter and derision. In this way, **sanctity has now become a "forgotten vision"**.

Forgotten, because once upon a time sanctity actually existed; because it was what inspired our civilization; because our people used to live among saints and they would draw from them the measure of their civilization; they were the heroes, the great champions, the "famous football players," and the "stars" of that time. Now, only the names of our saints remain, and even these have been "clipped" and altered in foreign fashion, while people now prefer to celebrate, instead of the memory of their saints, **their personal birthdays**. In times such as these, what can one say about sanctity? All words will fall on indifferent ears.

On the other hand, however, how can one not speak of a matter so central and fundamental to a Christian's life? Because without saints, our Faith is nonexistent; because if we leave out sanctity, there will be nothing left of the Church—only Her being identified with the world. Her "secularization" would be inevitable.

However, not only is sanctity "forgotten" in our day; it is also misinterpreted, whenever and however it is referred to. What is the significance of "sanctity", when one sees it as a portrayal of the Kingdom of God, as an experience and a foretasting of the eschaton?

MISAPPREHENDED SANCTITY

Should someone randomly ask people on the street what, in their opinion, "sanctity" is about, the reply they will hear as a rule is the following: a saint is the one who does not sin, one who upholds God's law, who is moral in every way—in short, someone sinless. Sometimes, an element of mysticism is added to the meaning of sanctity, according to which idea, a saint is one who possesses esoteric experiences, who communicates with the "divine," who falls into a trance and sees things that other people don't see—in other words, one who experiences supernatural situations and is able to perform supernatural acts.

In this way, the meaning of sanctity in people's minds appears to be linked to moralistic and psychological criteria. The more virtuous one is, the holier he is. And the more charismatic a person is, displaying abilities that people usually do not have (such as reading others' thoughts, foreseeing the future, etc.), the more this induces us to regard him as a "saint." The same applies reversely: when we discern a certain fault in someone's character or behavior (such as gluttony, anger, etc.), then we tend to write them off the "saint" list. Or, if someone does not display any supernatural abilities in one form or another, the thought alone that he could possibly be a saint, seems preposterous to us.

This common and widespread perception of sanctity gives rise to certain basic questions, when placed under the light of the Gospel, the Faith, and our Tradition. Let us mention some of them:

1. If sanctity is mainly about observing moral principles, then why was the Pharisee condemned by the Lord, whereas the tax-collector of the familiar parable was vindicated? We usually call the Pharisee a "hypocrite," but the fact is that he was not lying when he insisted that he faithfully upheld the Law, or that he gave one-tenth of his wealth to the poor, or that he did not omit to observe everything that the Lord demanded of him as a faithful Jew. He likewise was not lying when he characterized the tax-collector a sinner—as did the tax-collector himself—because the tax-collector was indeed unjust, and also a transgressor of moral rules.

2. A similar question also arises from the use of the word "saint" by the Apostle Paul in his Epistles. When addressing the Christians of Corinth, the Thessalonians, the Galatians, etc., Paul calls them "saints." However, further along in those Epistles, he points out the thousands of moral flaws of those Christians, which he censures most severely. In fact, in his Epistle to Galatians, it appears that the moral status of the "saints" there was so disappointing that Paul was compelled to write to them "If you bite and devour each other, take care that you do not exterminate each other!" So, how is it that the first Christians are referred to as "saints," when it is certain that their daily life did not conform to the requirements of their very Faith? I wonder, would anyone nowadays even consider calling any Christian a "saint"?

3. If sanctity is linked to supernatural charismas, then one would be able to seek it—and find it—outside the Church. It is a known fact that wicked spirits are equally capable of supernatural acts. Saints are not clairvoyants or fakirs, nor is their sanctity determined by such "charismas." There are saints of our Church for whom there is no mention of miracles; while there have been miracle-workers who have never been recognized as saints. Quite interesting are—respectively—the words of the Apostle Paul in his 1st Epistle to the Corinthians, who, like many today, were impressed by supernatural acts: ... *And if I have faith enough to move mountains, but have no love, then I am nothing* (1 Cor. 13:2). The Lord Himself had said that to command a mountain to move is possible, if you have faith *even as* (small as) *a mus-*

tard-seed (Mat. 17:20). But even this alone is not proof of sanctity; it is "nothing," if the prerequisite of love does not exist—in other words, if it is something that any person without miraculous capabilities can have. Miracle-working and sanctity do not relate to each other, nor do they necessarily co-exist.

4. Similar questions also arise, when sanctity is linked to unusual and "mystic" psychological experiences. Many people revert to oriental religions in order to meet with transcendental "gurus"— men of exceptional self-discipline, ascesis and prayer; however, our Church does not regard them as saints, regardless of how profound and supernatural their experiences may be, or how great their virtue may be.

Thus, the question is posed: **do saints exist, outside the Church?** If the word "saint" signifies that which people generally believe, as we described previously (that is, a moral lifestyle, supernatural charismas and supernatural experiences), then we will need to admit that "saints" do exist outside the Church (perhaps many more outside the Church, than inside it). If again we should wish to say that sanctity is possible only within the Church, then, **we must seek the meaning of "sanctity" beyond the criteria that we mentioned previously**—in other words, beyond moral perfection and supernatural powers and experiences.

So, let us see how our Church does perceive sanctity.

SANCTITY AS AN ECCLESIAL EXPERIENCE

The term "saint" has an interesting history. The root of this Hellenic word—(h)ágios—is in the fragment "**ag**," from which an entire series of terms are produced, such as "agnós" (=pure), "ágos" (=with positive inference, an object of religious reverence; with negative inference, a miasma, or curse). The deeper significance of this root is found in the verb "ἄζεσθαι" (pron.: á-zes-thae), which means to be in awe of a mystical and tremendous power (Aeschylus); also, the respect afforded to the bearer of Power (Homer, *Odyssey* 9200 e.a.) etc. Thus, in ancient Hellenism sanctity was linked to power; to that which Otto called "mysterium fascinosum et tremendum"—that which simultaneously inspired attraction and fear.

In the Old Testament, **the Semitic word** which was translated (into Greek) by the Septuagint Fathers as "saint" (hágios) is the word **qodesh**, which is closely related to the Assyrian word **kuddu-shu**, which means "**to sever, to separate**, to discern radically, to cleanse" (hence its linkage to cleanliness and chastity). Saintly things are those that are discerned from among the rest—mainly in worship—and are dedicated to God.

Thus, **the Holy Bible** goes beyond the psychological significance that we observe in the ancient Hellenes (awe, fear, respect towards a superior power) and **it links the notion of "saint" to an absolute otherness, to the absolute Other**—something that eventually leads the Holy Bible to link the term "saintly" (=holy) to God Himself—that is, to an absolute transcendence—when relating it to the world. Only God is "saintly" (holy), and therefore every sanctity springs from Him and from a relationship with Him.

In order to emphatically stress this belief, in the Old Testament Isaiah (the prophet of God's holiness) calls upon God three times: *Holy, holy, holy, is the Lord Sabaoth* (Is. 6:3) which in the Hebrew form of triple repetition signifies "infinitely holy" (compare to the 777 and its opposite, the 666, for which so much fuss and fear abounds nowadays).

Consequently, for the Holy Bible "sanctity" relates to God and not to any person or sacred article, as in ancient Hellenism; it becomes a persona, and in fact, with the Fathers of the Church it is linked to the Holy Trinity, with which the Fathers have related the Prophet Isaiah's "thrice-holy." **For the Christian faith, sanctity (holiness) is therefore not man-centered, but God-centered** and is not dependent on the moral achievements of Man—great though they may be—but on the glory and the grace of God and the degree of our personal relationship with the personal God. It is for this reason that the Holy Mother, the Theotokos, is named "Pan-agia" (all-saintly) or "Yper-agia" (supremely saintly): not on account of Her virtues, but because more than any other person in History, **she alone became personally united with the most holy God, by providing flesh and blood to the Son of God.**

For the Church, therefore, sanctity is not the personal property of any one person, no matter how "saintly" one may be in his lifetime; it has to do with one's personal relationship with God. God, according to His own free will, sanctifies whomever He chooses, without sanctity being dependent on anything else, other than the free will of the one being sanctified. As stressed by Saint Maximus the Confessor, **we people do not contribute anything, except only our willingness**, without which God will not act; furthermore, our labors and ascesis do not produce sanctity as a result thereof, as they can be proven to be worthless chaff.

In the Christian faith, this relating of sanctity to God Himself leads to its linking to the very glory of God. Sanctity-holiness now means the glorification of God by the entire world. It is not perchance that the primary request in the Lord's Prayer is: "hallowed be Thy Name." If we stop to consider that this prayer is eschatological—that is, it refers to the final state of the world—it is obvious that what we ask for in the Lord's Prayer is for God to be glorified by all the world; for the moment to come when all the world will cry out together with the Cherubim what Isaiah saw and heard in his vision: "Holy, holy, holy, is the Lord Sabaoth; replete are the heavens and the earth with Your glory! Hosanna, to the One on high!"

The saints do not seek any personal glory, but the glory of God. God glorifies the saints, not with their own glory, but with **His** glory. The saints are sanctified and glorified, not with a sanctity and a glory that springs from within them, but **with the sanctity and the glory of God Himself** (notice how Byzantine iconography depicts the light as being directed externally, onto and into the subjects portrayed). This is of special significance for the theosis of the saints.

As elucidated during the hesychast arguments of the 14th century and contrary to Western theology which spoke of "created" grace (i.e., that grace and glory belong to the very nature of Man, as supposedly given by God during Creation), Orthodox theology –as **developed by Saint Gregory Palamas and the other hesychasts of that era**—perceives the light that the saints see, as well as the glory that envelops them, as the "uncreated" energies of God; that is, as the light and the glory of God Himself. A true saint is the one who does not seek personal glory in any way, but only the glory of God. When one seeks personal glory he loses his sanctity, because in the long run, none other is holy except God. **Sanctity-holiness** involves a partaking and communing of God's holiness; after all, that is what "theosis" (deification) means. **Any sanctity that hinges on our virtues, our morality, our qualifications, our ascetic labors, etc. is demonic**, and has nothing to do with the sanctity of our Church. From these observations, it becomes obvious that the source of sanctity-holiness par excellence is found in the Divine Eucharist. Let us elaborate somewhat on this position.

We have said that there is no other sanctity-holiness other than that of God, and that the saints do not possess any sanctity of their own, but partake of God's sanctity-holiness. This means that in the Church, we do not have saints, except only in the sense of those who have been sanctified.

When, during the 4th century A.D., discussions were taking place on the subject of the divinity of the Holy Spirit, the main argument presented by saint Athanasius to prove that the Holy Spirit is God and not a creation, was that the Holy Spirit cannot be sanctified, instead, He sanctifies. If the Holy Spirit could be sanctified, then He would indeed be a creation, because creations—and consequently humans—do not sanctify; they are sanctified.

In His Magisterial prayer, as preserved in John's Gospel and cited in the first of the "twelve gospel readings" of Great Thursday, Christ utters this meaningful phrase to the Father: *For their sake* (=the disciples, and by extension, all people) *do I sanctify Myself, so that they too may in truth be sanctified* (John 17:19).These words were spoken just prior to the Passion, and, when related to the Last Supper, they acquire a Eucharistic meaning: with His sacrifice, Christ Himself (as God) sanctifies Himself (as a human), so that we humans may be sanctified through Communion of His Body and His Blood. With our participation in the Divine Eucharist, we are sanctified; that is, **we become saints by partaking of the one and only Holy** ("saintly") **One: Christ**.

Perhaps in a Christian's life there is no point as revealing (as to what sanctity is), than the moment when the priest raises up the Precious Body prior to Holy Communion, saying: "**The sanctified** (the holy Body) **unto the sanctified** (the saints)"—in other words, the sanctified (holy) Body of Christ and His Blood are now being offered to the sanctified ones (the "saints"), the members of the

Church, for communion. The response of the laity following these words is overwhelming (inasmuch as it summarizes everything that we said previously): "**One (only) is Holy, One is the Lord: Jesus Christ, in glorification of God the Father.**" Only one is actually holy: Jesus Christ. We all are sinners. And His sanctity-holiness does not aspire to anything else except the glorification of God ("in glorification of God the Father...."). **It is at that precise moment that the Church experiences sanctity-holiness at its apex.** By confessing that "One is Holy," every single virtue of ours and every worth vanish before the sanctity-holiness of the Only Holy One. This does not mean that we can approach Holy Communion without any prior preparation and labor for a worthy approach. It does however imply that no matter how much we may prepare ourselves, we do not become saints before having received Communion. **Sanctity does not precede Eucharistic communion; it follows it.** If we are saints prior to receiving Holy Communion, then what is the purpose of Holy Communion? Only our participation in the sanctity-holiness of our God sanctifies us, and that is what Holy Communion offers us.

From this observation springs a series of truths that are relevant to our subject:

The first one is that in this way, we can comprehend why—as mentioned earlier along in our homily—in the Epistles of the Apostle Paul all the members of the Church are referred to as "saints," **despite the fact that they were not characterized by moral perfection.** Given that "sanctity"—as regards the people—connotes a partaking of God's sanctity-holiness in the manner that it is offered by Christ, Who sanctifies Himself with His Sacrifice, then all the members of the Church who participate in that sanctification can be called "saints".

By the same token, ever since the first centuries of the Church, all the elements used in the Eucharist have also been given the name "holies" (the "sanctified," as above: "the sanctified unto the sanctified"), even though by nature they are not holy. And it is for the same reason that the Church bestowed at an early stage the title of "saint" to the Bishops. Many people are scandalized nowadays when we say "the saint (so and so)". For example, a certain reporter whose main job was to publicize the scandals of bishops, had intentionally printed the word "saint" placed inside quotation marks, before the bishop's name. Bishops are addressed in this manner, not as an indication of their virtues, but because in the Divine Eucharist it is they who portray the Only Holy One; they are the ones who are images of Christ, who are standing in the place and in the manner of God, according to Saint Ignatius. **It is the place of the Bishop in the Divine Eucharist that justifies the title of "saint."** Before undergoing the corruption of pietism, the Orthodox had no difficulty whatsoever with the terminology of portrayals, and would "see" Christ Himself in the person of the one who was portraying Him during the Divine Liturgy, that is: the bishop.

Thus, the Divine Eucharist is the "communion of saints" par excellence. That is what the labors of the ascetics aspire to, which labors are never the end, but only the means towards the end, which is Eucharistic communion. This point is forgotten and overlooked by many contemporary theologians, even Orthodox ones, who especially in our day tend to relate sanctity to ascetic labours.

The case of Saint Mary of Egypt is an eloquent example. For forty entire years, she labored ascetically in the desert with all her might in order to be cleansed of her former passions/sins, but only when she received the Communion of the Immaculate Gifts from the saint did her earthly life come to an end, having then become sanctified. The aim of her ascesis was Eucharistic Communion. Would Mary have been a saint, if she had been cleansed of passions, but had not received Holy Communion? The answer is most probably no.

However, the Divine Eucharist is the culmination of sanctification, not only because it offers Man the most perfect and fullest union (physical and spiritual) with the Only Holy One, but also because it comprises the most perfect portrayal of the Kingdom of God; that is, the state in which all of Creation will be eternally and incessantly praising and glorifying the "holy, holy, holy, is the Lord Sabaoth."

From the book Sanctity: A Forgotten Vision
(Athens: Akritas publications).
Source: Piraiki Ecclesia, *no. 187, Nov. 2007, pp. 2–7.*
Republished by the blog: Manitaritoubounou.

HERE
ENDS THE BOOK,
"TO THE GLORY OF GOD
THE FATHER": THE LIVES OF
SAINT MARDARIJE OF LIBERTYVILLE
AND SAINT SEBASTIAN OF JACKSON AND
THEIR SELECTED WRITINGS, PROLOGUED
BY HIS HOLINESS SERBIAN PATRIARCH IRINEJ,
COMPOSED BY THE EDITORS: BISHOP MAXIM
(VASILJEVIĆ), HIEROMONK DAMASCENE
(CHRISTENSEN), AND PRESBYTERA RUŽICA MARIĆ;
TRANSLATED BY HIEROMONK SERAFIM (BALTIĆ)
AND DEACON MARKO BOJOVIĆ, ILLUSTRATED
BY WORKS OF THE ICONOGRAPHER MILOJE
MILINKOVIĆ; THIS EDITION IS LIMITED TO 2000
COPIES AND WAS PUBLISHED IN ALHAMBRA,
CALIFORNIA, WITH THE BLESSING OF THE
EPISCOPAL COUNCIL OF THE SERBIAN
ORTHODOX CHURCH IN NORTH AND SOUTH
AMERICA, SUPPORTED BY THE CLERGY
BROTHERHOOD OF THIS CHURCH,
PRINTED AT THE INTERKLIMA-
GRAFIKA PRESS IN VRNJCI, SERBIA,
OWNED BY KYR LJUBIŠA
ČEPERKOVIĆ, REALIZED
BY SEBASTIAN PRESS
IN LOS ANGELES, CA,
AND FINISHED ON
THE 30TH DAY OF
JULY, IN THE YEAR
OF THE LORD 2015.
THIS COPY IS NUMBER

1535